"A GRATEFUL NA[TION] SOON FORGO[T]"

BY JOHN LEE

THE CONVOY WAR STORY OF SOUTHEND PIER

Dedicated to the memory of
John Pelham Champion, CBE., DSO., RN

ISBN 978-1-3999-4960-6

Book design, layout and production management by Into Print
www.intoprint.net
+44 (0)1604 832140

THE CONVOY WAR STORY OF SOUTHEND PIER

Here at the gateway to the River Thames in Southend came together more merchant ships' masters and the greatest number of convoys sailed than ever in the history of the world

84,297 ships sailed in convoys from Southend Pier 1939 - 1945

"A GRATEFUL NATION SOON FORGOT"

It was the great A. P. Herbert (Sir Alan Herbert), when giving his first-hand account of Naval Control Service operations in Southend-on-Sea throughout WWII, who wrote "A Grateful Nation Soon Forgot". A. P. Herbert, in a 32 page booklet written for the Southend Corporation in 1945, was referring to the momentous contribution of Southend in defence of the nation at the most important time in its history. The foreword to his booklet is a tribute to Southend by A. V. Alexander, First Lord of the Admiralty.

The Naval Control Service Southend was given the shore base name HMS Leigh. The Southend base was a strategic location for a service with worldwide significance.

On 21st October, 1939 the Nazi propagandist known as Lord Haw Haw, in his famous radio broadcast "Germany Calling, Germany Calling" addressed directly the people of Southend. **"The Luftwaffe is coming"**

On a hunch, Capt. Champion, Officer in Charge Naval Control Services Southend, predicted the attack on Southend Pier by the Luftwaffe as the first clear night, 22nd November, 1939

The Pier was defended and the Luftwaffe thwarted. The River Thames and access to the nation's capital stayed open for the duration of the war, contrary to Churchill's stated belief that it would have to close.

Has one man's hunch ever had greater consequences in the defence of a nation?

D-Day preparations including 32 U.S. Navy Ships at the Pier

Brexit Irony. Don't Mention the War.

Some Selected Character Profiles

Index

I found the A. P. Herbert 1945 booklet at a jumble sale many years ago and it became my inspiration for research. That research was to result in me acquiring some rare and valuable documents now in my possession which bring to life the day to day events over six years of a vital period in the nation's and Southend's history. The impact of A. P. Herbert's heartfelt plea for recognition of Southend's part in the war was telling on me, giving great pride, as one born and bred in this seaside town, once known as 'the playground of London's East End'.

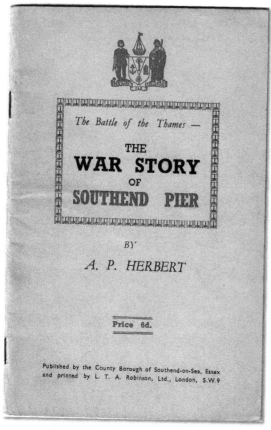

The booklet written by A. P. Herbert for Southend Corporation in 1945

I was mystified. Why was so little known or spoken about this important period in our history? Local historians have made only short passing reference to what was clearly a time of great events.

I procrastinated for years, undecided how to shine a light on Southend's unsung heroic story. Eventually in 2009, and again later, I made approaches to members and leaders of Southend Council. There was no real interest. Southend Council's concentration was on changing people's perception of the town and creating their 'City of Culture'. I wrote to Her Majesty the Queen in 2011 enclosing my 1945 copy of A. P. Herbert's booklet but unfortunately linked the timing to coincide with Southend's bid, in competition with other towns, for the award of city status in Her Majesty's Diamond Jubilee year. I received a reply from Her Majesty thanking me and stating that my letter had been passed to the Cabinet Office and placed with Southend's papers in support of their bid which predictably was unsuccessful. I mentioned to Her Majesty that Prince Philip had been an officer aboard destroyer H.M.S. Wallace as a leading convoy escort down the East Coast route in the early days of convoy operations. It was a battle zone known as 'Bomb Alley', and I am sure by lots more unprintable naval terms, because of the extent of German attacks on our convoys by sea and by air. Early convoys were exceptionally vulnerable as there was little air cover until after the Battle of Britain. Prince Philip's convoy escort duties suggest he may well have trod the boards of Southend Pier.

My letter to Her Majesty was read out in the Southend Council chamber by the late Gwen Horrigan, Councillor and a former Mayor of Southend. Gwen was a lone supporter at that time of my campaign for there to be at least some proper local recognition.

Also in September of 2011, my friend Emma Wynne Morgan, who produces the local monthly publication 'Oracle', printed an article by me. At the end of it I made a plea to the public for any additional information I could obtain. For me the principal character in overseeing 6 years of historic and momentous events on behalf of the nation in wartime, was Captain John Pelham Champion, CBE., DSO., RN. I could never have imagined that a delightful lady in Leigh-on-Sea who read the article would contact me stating that her sister, Rita Barham, had been Capt. Champion's secretary throughout the war years. A visit to Rita (then in her 90's) at her home in Norfolk was to reveal a goldmine of first-hand information and unique memorabilia.

Rita remembered John Champion as a very kind man and enjoyed her years of working for him. When HMS Leigh was de-commissioned in 1945, having been promoted to Commodore-in-Charge on 1st January 1944, John Champion wrote a very good letter of reference for Rita which she kept with her papers from that time.

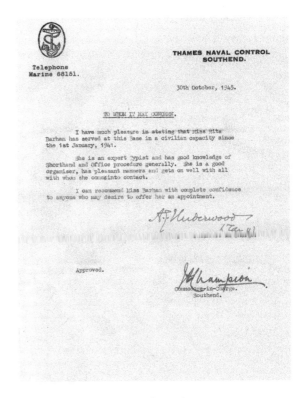

Commodore-in-Charge Naval Control Services Southend, John Pelham Champion, CBE., DSO., RN

At the end of the war Commodore Champion created a log for the War Office of the six years of events and statistics entitled "SOUTHEND AND THAMES NAVAL CONTROL IN WAR 1939 - 1945". This document contains the most important record but was not allowed for release until 1972 under War Office restrictions. A copy is available from Naval Records, Kew under reference Adm 199 No. 2174 - supplement B to Volume 26. This log records NCS activities with wide international connections.

Rita's glowing reference

Rita described John Champion as "a very kind man". Kind he may have been but also a disciplinarian for sure. NCS Southend could not have succeeded without a strict code of discipline.

A ship's Master, brought to book for a breach of orders, accused the Captain of being a "Martinet".

A disciplinary matter with different outcome was when one night a patrol boat came alongside a collier ordering the collier to put out an offending masthead light which should not have been showing. There was an electrical fault and the obstinate light continued to glow. There was only one thing to do; take a revolver and shoot it out. Next morning the collier's Master was told to report to Captain Champion's office for a rollicking. When the Master walked in Captain Champion looked up and was puzzled. "Don't I know you?" he said. "You should do" replied the Master. "I've been on every other Channel Convoy since 1940".

The Master was questioned closely on how many trips he had made – it was 60 or 70 and Captain Champion exploded. "Good God, I've decorated men for doing four trips to the North Coast." The Master was given a cup of coffee and within a short while received an M.B.E. The masthead light was tactfully forgotten

An Ideal Facility

Southend Pier stretches for a mile and one-third out into the Thames Estuary which widens towards the North Sea. The pier railway runs for one and a quarter miles of its length. In peacetime, the longest pleasure pier in the world had great entertainment facilities and traditional 'end of the pier' variety shows and big band orchestra concerts. The Solarium was a theatre decked out with cardboard cut-outs of palm trees and tropical themes. Because of a deep water harbour at the end of the pier there were regular steamship cruises over to France, or shorter day trips up river or across to Kent and the River Medway.

From 1939 – 1945 no fewer than 84,297 ships sailed in 3,367 convoys from the end of Southend Pier via the Thames Estuary and that long and difficult to navigate sandbank known as The Nore, to the North Sea. The end of pier Solarium became the convoy conference room. Southend would have the company of great and distinguished naval men who came back into the service from retirement. These included Admirals, Vice Admirals and Battle of Jutland veterans. All men of valour, experience and a knowledge of seamanship second to none. Their task was to help Southend's Naval Control Service in the organisation and command of convoy operations destined to face attack by air, especially from German Stuka dive bombers, and by sea with U-boat submarines and E.boat fast attack craft as well as the mining of our waters and convoy routes.

The permanent working craft of trawlers, drifters, salvage vessels and tugs included a force of men from many different nations. Some of the Sun Tugs (work horses) were crewed by Americans.

Although NCS Southend was answerable to HQ Chatham, there was vital liaison with Commander in Chief The Nore, who had more direct control over the convoy work of the Southend base. C in C The Nore had heavy operational responsibility for the control of convoys and vast minesweeping tasks carried out by NCS Southend.

Commander in Chief The Nore had for centuries been a title given only to Admirals. There were four such Admirals in post from 1939 - 1945 as C in C The Nore. All had their special relationship with Naval Control Services Southend. Admiral Studholme Brownrigg KBE., CB., DSO was in place for only the first few months of the war and was succeeded by Admiral The Hon. Sir Reginald Plunket-Ernle-Erle Drax KCB., DSO until 1941. He visited NCS Southend on 7th March 1940 and his frequent messages of congratulations for the work of the NCS at Southend are on record. From 1941 C in C The Nore was Admiral George Lyon KCB and finally Admiral 1st Baron Sir John Tovey GCB., KBE., DSO. A further additional and vital involvement for Admiral Tovey was the build-up for D-Day and the invasion of Normandy.

Complex planning of convoy operations lasted for six years. According to A. P. Herbert "Every convoy was a joint masterpiece by the Port and the Navy". That was not all. Large scale emergency operations were mounted in Southend for the evacuation of Dunkirk. Assistance was given with PLUTO the undersea pipeline to France and TURCO (Turnaround Control Operation). TURCO required altering operating procedures and the introduction of complicated communication systems in preparing vessels for their departure to Normandy. This included assembling hundreds of craft carrying soldiers of British, American and other nationalities departing from Southend on 5th June 1944 for the D-Day assault in Normandy. The day before their departure there were 203 ships of every kind loaded with men and arms at Southend. Most were British and American. Over 50 small craft were needed to marshall and serve the emergency demands of a large scattered fleet. By next morning they had all left safely.

4

In Phase 1 of the build-up to D-Day from 1st March to 10th June 1944 no fewer than 836 minor war vessels were sailed from Southend in groups. These comprised Landing Craft LCT's, LC2's, LCV's as well as Trawlers, MOB's, Tids, VIC's and tugs. In Phase 2 and the larger build-up there was enormous pressure on NCS staff. American motor boats / PBR's were attracted to the pier like a magnet. Their respective authorities had neglected to make proper preparations and provisions for victualling. There was a lack of 'gear' to make the vessels seaworthy for their passage. NCS Southend made them ready.

Large casements to make up the Mulberry Harbours at Arromanches and Omaha beaches, to facilitate the landing of huge numbers of vehicles and military equipment, sailed down The Thames passed the pier. They were floated out to sea and across the Channel to Normandy where they were assembled. One casement sunk before leaving the Thames Estuary and is still visible off Shoeburyness. Towards the end of the war a task force of ships manned by British, Canadians and Poles sailed from Southend to Belgium where they successfully cleared the River Scheldte of Germans, opening a route through Antwerp to the Dutch ports. This event is recorded on a plaque at the end of a short pier on the Scheldte in Antwerp.

Supply convoys over land and sea in wartime have always been essential to feeding the population, the powering of industries and the mobility of fighting forces.

Germany was observing Southend Pier and its potential for convoy duties long before the war. It recognised, as did The War Department, who were in consultation with Southend Corporation as far back as 1936, the strategic importance of Southend and the Pier. Not only does it stand at the gateway to the Thames and London but it is close to the North Sea and East Coast supply routes.

Captain Champion wished it to be known the importance of Trinity House Pilots from the Trade Division be recognised. Captain Ellison was a Pilot Officer who attached himself to Southend and apart from other services personally piloted 800 small

vessels as an example of the kind of cooperation received by NCS Southend. Thames Pilots rendered "splendid service" to the country. Ruler of Pilots, Captain Owen invariably cooperated "in the most friendly manner" with the navy throughout the war.

Painting of an East Coast Convoy at Southend in 1942 by N. Southeby Pitcher. This painting was commissioned by Delphine Tatham a Wren whose father was a Lieut. Commander. From 1947 - 1977 Delphine worked for GCHQ

William Joyce (Lord Haw Haw) addresses the people of Southend directly in one of his early Nazi propaganda broadcasts "Germany calling. Germany calling"

On 21st October 1939, only weeks after war was declared, William Joyce (Lord Haw Haw) in one of his 'Germany Calling' propaganda broadcasts, addressed the people of Southend directly with these words:

"You people of Southend boast that you have the longest pier in the world. I can assure you that by Monday it will be the shortest".

I first discovered the words of this broadcast as reported in The Glasgow Herald newspaper and printed next day. I have since found the same was also reported in The Southend Standard at that time.

This would be one of many such propaganda broadcasts throughout the war. When eventually captured Joyce was brought back to England, tried and hanged.

I have attributed this early Lord Haw Haw broadcast to Wm. Joyce with whose name these broadcasts were soon to become synonymous. However, Joyce, after fleeing to Germany from England in August 1939, joined Joseph Goebbels' Nazi propaganda ministry in September. Initially he was used as a news reader in English. In the October address to the people of Southend It is possible that Lord Haw Haw was in fact Norman Baillie-Stewart a disaffected ex-Scottish Seaforth Highland officer with long time German sympathies. At that time a 'haw haw' type was one who spoke in a posh, pompous and haughty manner. A bit like a Joyce Grenfell female version shouting "Jolly Hockey Sticks!". There were also rumours that the person could even have been the fine English speaking German called Wolf Mittler. Interest in who the broadcaster was became the subject of much press speculation and publicity by Lord Beaverbrook in his newspapers. His papers promoted a guessing game. For many the broadcasts were compulsive listening with whole families tuning in nightly on their wireless sets.

Often there would be mention of a British soldier by name with a message to his wife or family. Apart from trying to instill fear, Joyce would also make false statements on statistics of British planes shot down. These were always exaggerated with a final claim that all German planes returned safely.

Lord Haw Haw's warning to the people of Southend was no idle boast. The intention of the Germans was to remove this vital wartime supplies lifeline they knew was so important. Britain needed to continue essential supplies, including to countless industries along the River Thames to London, where the capital, the seat of Government and our War Cabinet operated.

Winston Churchill had stated that he thought that the River Thames would have to be closed. If the timing of a threatened attack in that broadcast was wrong there was no doubting that the Germans had a plan to destroy Southend Pier and its marshalling facility for convoy shipping.

A. P. Herbert was present when Churchill made his River Thames prediction. He wrote as follows: "Late on the last night the House of Commons met before the War, I said to Mr. Churchill. "Do you think there will be a war, sir?" "Yes" he answered, "Without question." Then he added without a cue from anyone "I think we shall have to abandon the Thames".

The River Thames at this time was the route to the busiest ports in the world. Tilbury and Gravesend are 15 miles up-river from Southend; the Royal Docks at Woolwich 31 miles; East India Docks 35; Surrey Commercial Docks 38 and London Docks 39 miles. From these docks one quarter of the population was supplied. 60 million tons of shipping came in and out of those ports every year before the war.

It cannot be stressed enough how important coal was at this time. All of industry was dependent on coal fuel. Steam trains ran on coal. Coal fired power stations produced electricity for industrial and domestic lighting. Coal was used to keep fires burning in every home for heat. Along the East Coast the main supplies of coal came from Scotland and Newcastle. Wartime stockpiles of coal were everywhere and sometimes in the most unusual places.

Gan for ever, last coal from Newcastle...

THE last ever shipment of coal from Newcastle left the Tyne shortly before midnight last night, bringing centuries of North East history to an end.

The ship Longwave loaded its final 12,000-ton cargo from Tyneside, which has exported coal since the 13th century.

By 1913, the Great North Coal Field employed 250,000 and produced 55million tons a year. The huge scale of the industry led to the phrase 'carrying coals to Newcastle' to describe a pointless task.

Although the end of coal-fired power stations slashed demand, coal is still used to make steel, glass and cement.

An article in the Daily Mail of 19th February 2021 announcing the last ever shipment of coal from Newcastle

Establishing the Naval Control Service (silk purse from sow's ear)

On 29th September 1938, only 35 miles upstream from Southend, things began with the establishment of the Naval Control Service (NCS) with a sub base at Southend. In the summer of the following year, Rear Admiral E. C. Boyle, VC., RN., as FOIC (Flag Officer in Charge) London, set up headquarters at the Port of London Authority building near Tower Hill. On 25th August 1939 the navy took over Southend Pier. The intention was to run the show from London but this soon proved impractical. The idea was for ships to be instructed and routed in London and to sail independently down The Thames, out past the historic Nore sandbank to the The North Sea. They could be contacted at Southend in an emergency.

A lady walks her dog through Regents Park and past the stockpiles of coal stored there during the war

A convoy assembly anchorage in Southend had not been part of the original plan.

Naval Officer Captain R. V. Alison, DSO., RN was allocated the task of consulting with ports, docks, shipping authorities and with the Admiralty Trade Division in controlling operations. Roger Vincent Alison, born in Glastonbury, was now 54 years of age and taken out of retirement. A WWI Battle of Jutland veteran, Alison was mentioned in despatches for bravery. In WWII the task given to him was impossible. He had to convince his superiors that a better option would be to create at Southend a convoy shipping facility. It is incredible that in the run up to the war there had been no proper planning for supplies in and out of the country and that an obvious facility like that in Southend at the gateway to The Thames had been overlooked except by the Germans. Capt. Alison now moved to Southend to join Naval Officer in Charge there, Capt. E. H. Martin RN who had fallen sick and by December was invalided out of the service. He was immediately replaced by Captain A. S. May, MVO., DSO., RN.

Southend was not ready. It was understaffed and lacking in every facility including being devoid of boarding craft and communication systems / equipment. The situation was desperate and demanded drastic measures. Nevertheless on 7th September 1939, four days after the outbreak of war, the first convoys were sailed. The following signal in acknowledgement was received from the Admiralty on 13th September 1939. *"The expeditious organisation of convoys A,B,C is a matter of much satisfaction to their Lordships and reflects great credit on all concerned."*

For the first two months the switchboard was manned by RNVR signals ratings and local pensioners. A volunteer messenger service was provided by local Sea Scouts! During November 1939 a vital teleprinter was installed with a direct line to HMS Pembroke, the shore base name of HQ Chatham. Services at the anchorage could not be maintained without proper communication facilities and approval was obtained for Boarding Craft to be supplied with radio telephones.

The first shore station at Southend was established in the Palace Hotel overlooking the Pier. It was manned by ordinary seamen RNVR. Using plain language for radio telephone communication was out of the question but there was no suitable code in existence. NCS Southend created a code and cypher training in its use. This became the adopted code language throughout all UK NCS bases.

During the whole of this early period, the Flag Officer in Charge London, Rear Admiral Boyle and Naval Control Service Officer Thames, Capt. Alison, were at odds. They did not see eye to eye and serious differences let to bitter argument. In short, the difficulty was that merchant shipping operated under the rules of the Board of Trade and Royal Navy shipping under the Admiralty. This separation of controls put members with a common interest into conflict. As a result a conference was held at the Admiralty, chaired by Rear Admiral H.M. Burrough. Capt. Alison won the day and a unified command was established with NCS Southend answerable to Chatham HQ and to Commander in Chief The Nore. This was the start of creating a successful NCS operation at Southend subject to a quick learning curve and tremendous hard work. Capt. Alison is credited with setting things up at the new Southend base before he was replaced by the appropriately named Captain Champion. The unified command was to significantly improve operations in the coming years. Without it Southend's great contribution to the support for D-Day preparations would have been impossible.

It is said that "cometh the hour, cometh the man". This is surely an appropriate epithet for one Captain John Pelham Champion, CBE., DSO., RN., who was to command NCS operations in Southend from 14th October 1939 throughout the war, apart from the few months September 1940 - April 1941, when he was Naval Officer in Charge, Liverpool.

A vicar's son from Edale in Derbyshire, John Pelham Champion at age not yet 14 joined the Naval Training Ship Britannia at Dartmouth. Three months earlier at the same age and as a contemporary in training with John Champion was

Andrew Browne Cunningham, later to become Admiral of the Fleet, 1st Viscount Lord Cunningham of Hyndhope.

John Pelham Champion's DSO., was won as Captain of the destroyer 'Maenad' at the Battle of Jutland for heroic action whilst leader of 2nd Division 12th Destroyer Flotilla. After WWI John Champion retired to the village of Hasketon in Suffolk, near Woodbridge, and continued sailing as a hobby. When the call came for volunteer WWII duty he was first sent to Nova Scotia to be part of an escort for the first convoy (HX1) out of Halifax, across the Atlantic to Liverpool. His escort vessel was the heavy cruiser HMS Berwick. Soon afterwards he was given the almighty challenge of controlling convoy operations at Southend.

Temporary accommodation was reserved for most Naval Control Service officers in the Palace Hotel opposite the entrance to the pier. Requirements expanded until NCS officers dominated occupation of the hotel.

At the beginning the officers and ratings of Thames Naval Control were borne on the books of land base HMS Pembroke IV at HQ Chatham. On 1st October 1941 'HMS Leigh' was commissioned as the shore base title for Southend. All naval control staff were transferred in an act that combined operations under a unified command that greatly facilitated the organisation of the NCS in the Thames.

Georgian Royal Terrace

It was no coincidence that Captain Champion chose as his HQ Nos. 7, 8 and 9 Royal Terrace, high up overlooking Southend Pier, where he flew his broad pennant and the white ensign and a stone's throw from the Palace Hotel. John Champion had a great sense of history for it was here at Nos 7, 8 and 9 in this row of Georgian Houses that Nelson is said to have made romantic visits to Lady Emma Hamilton his mistress. These three houses were also occupied on several occasions by Princess Caroline who in 1803 stayed there to 'take the waters'. At this point the Thames Estuary becomes a wide salt water river where it meets the influx from the North Sea. Bathing in the sea at Southend became very popular in Georgian times. It was whilst staying at this address with her illegitimate daughter Horatia in 1805 that Lady Hamilton received the news of Nelson's death at Trafalgar. A ball in Nelson's honour was arranged by Lady Hamilton in the Royal Hotel at the end of Royal Terrace. Looking at the Royal Hotel today it does not take much to imagine those celebrations of over 200 years ago.

Requisitioning and Evacuation

Suddenly the seafront amusement arcades and entertainment establishments so popular with East End day trippers were closed. 'Kiss me quick' hats and Southend rock were replaced by military uniforms and 'hard tack'.

As the NCS was being established in Southend word went out to boat owners and yachtsmen the length of the Thames to volunteer their craft for the River Emergency Services in patrolling The Thames from Hammersmith to Southend. A. P. Herbert in Teddington was one of those whose boat was requisitioned for the service.

Two thirds of Southend's population was evacuated at the beginning of the war in the knowledge that Southend would be a target for bombing, as indeed it was. I was born in March 1939 in a road leading to Southend seafront not 200 yards away. My sister aged 5 had been compulsorily evacuated to a family at Sutton in Ashfield,

Nottinghamshire. My father, a merchant seaman all his working life, until meeting my mother in 1934, had been volunteering for service but rejected on account of his age. In 1939 he was aged 30. He was accepted into the army in 1941 or 1942. On 6th June 1944 he arrived on Juno beach as part of the D-Day landings.

As a babe in arms, with my father, my mother, my maternal grandmother and my aunt Ellen (married to my father's brother who was in the merchant navy) we all moved to Mansfield in Nottinghamshire. My somewhat rebellious 5 years old evacuated sister, only 3 miles away at Sutton in Ashfield was brought back into the family. She was not liked by the people she was with, especially after she decided that their black spotted Dalmatian dog should be black all over, and covered it with boot polish.

My father and my aunt Ellen worked for BSA in their ball bearing factory making munitions. There was more danger here in Mansfield than living in Southend. After a couple of years, like many others who returned, we decided to move back. Meanwhile Southend had filled up with army and naval military personnel.

We returned to the area we had left, occupying first one empty property where the owners were absent and then another, wherever my father managed to gain entry. Then in about 1941 we found proper rented accommodation in Stadium Road, Southend. Opposite the houses in Stadium Road were high fences and walls behind which was a greyhound stadium. The field in the centre of the racing track was Southend United F.C's home pitch. The stadium at this time had been taken over by military and was installed with search lights used to pinpoint German aircraft on their frequent bombing raids. Sirens and searchlights for us were a part of everyday life. This was the time of 'blackout'. Everyone had to put up black curtains and avoid any sign of light. There were no street lights and movement around the streets was by

Soldiers who were billeted in Stadium and surrounding roads just before the unit's departure.
See my sister and me squeezed in on the right.

10

using a torch pointed to the ground. As children we could distinguish between the droning sounds of large aircraft. "It is one of ours" or "It is one of theirs". Stadium Road and some houses in adjoining streets were part occupied by soldiers. We got to know many of them. Their canteen facilities were a series of large Nissan huts in the stadium's car park at the end of the road just yards from No. 4 were we lived. In about 1943 the troops left (we believe for Italy) and in a group photograph taken before they departed, a solder we knew as 'Curly', pulled my sister Peggie and me into the side. It is a treasured photograph of Peggie aged 8 and me aged 4 on the end of our occupying troops.

The Convoys

On 7th September 1939 just four days after the declaration of war the first two convoys sailed from Southend Pier. These were the very first convoys of the war. Convoys were allocated code letters for established route names. From Southend FN convoys were bound for Forth North and on return FS for Forth South to the East Coast ports at Southend and Ramsgate. An OA convoy was Outbound on route A. CW was Channel Westbound and CE was Channel Eastbound, all destined for the Atlantic. After their code letters convoy sailings were numbered in chronological sequence.

On 7th September 1939 FN1 left Southend for Methil in Scotland with 19 ships in the convoy and Vice Admiral Lane Poole as Commodore in S.S. Hetton. Sir Richard Hayden Owen Lane-Poole KBE, CB., held high naval office until his retirement just before the war. Coming out of retirement Lane Poole served as a commodore of convoys and as 'Director of Demagnetization' as an expert on magnetic mines. This last working title was no doubt due to the experience he could bring from his time at the Mining School in Portsmouth followed by valuable knowledge of mines and mine laying operations during WW1. On 1st January 1944 he was advanced to Knight Commander of the Order of the British Empire. Here on 7th September 1939 he acted not as a Vice Admiral but as a Commodore, leading the way on this first East Coast convoy in the small steamship collier SS. Hetton!

On the same day, OA1 left with 17 ships led by Vice Admiral Dawson as Commodore in S.S. Gloucester Castle, sometimes referred to as "Go Slow Coaster". This convoy was escorted by destroyer HMS Antelope to the Atlantic where she was 'buttoned' (joined) by 10 more ships out of Liverpool. The first destination was Sierra Leone with final destination Halifax Nova Scotia. Ironically Captain Champion had set sail as escort for HX1 from Halifax to Liverpool on 16th September. HX1 passed OA1 en-route. Sadly it was in July 1942 that the S.S. Gloucester Castle was bombed and sunk off Sierra Leone with the loss of most of her crew including her master.

If organising a convoy sounds simple it was anything but. The ships had first to be assembled in 'the roads' by an appointed time. Their pilots were taken off and the ship's masters must be brought ashore for a conference. There were many matters to be discussed and problems to be thrashed out involving the Commodores of the convoys and their Escort Commanders. Ships varied in power and speed and a common speed had to be established. Their routes were determined by latest information on minefields, wrecked ships, sand banks and prowling German E-boats. They must weigh anchor at given times and proceed through narrow waters to take up formation. Other instructions were received by signalling codes communicated by flags, sirens and flashing lights. After convoy conferences, held in the pre-war end of pier entertainment 'Sun Room', decorated with those cut-out palm trees and tropical themes, the Masters had to be returned to their ships which could be lying up to 5 miles away. Every captain during six years of operations was safely put aboard his ship. The pier railway ran at all hours of the day and night throughout the war. Apart from the continual traffic travelling to and from the shore, the trains carried sick and injured soldiers returned from battle. Others besides the navy were busy on the pier. 200 army pioneers lived on the pier in the first few months of the war, building all sorts of defences including pill boxes, rocket launchers and they laid demolition charges in case of the need to scuttle!

Mona Budd - Caterer extraordinary

In his booklet, AP mentioned a woman known only as "Mona". Firstly we have AP's own words followed by recent research to determine who Mona was.

Page 7 of "The War Story of Southend Pier by A. P. Herbert"

"Last but not least, we must remember the catering contractor on the Pier, who through all the war, kept the café and food stores going, supplied the Pier Head and, at need, the ships and as one high officer said, "made all things possible." He was supported by the good lady affectionately

known as Mona to Masters of the Merchant Navy all over the world, for her efficient handling of the feeding arrangements in the café. On one occasion there were fifty ships off the Pier for five days, held up by mining outside, and short of food. On this and other occasions, as when the little ships were calling at Southend Pier en route for Dunkirk, the catering staff worked night and day and rendered an indispensable service. N.A.A.F.I. of course could not be employed as they cannot serve civilians."

As Mona has been immortalised by the great A. P. Herbert, more about this lady became a subject for research. Heather Feather, HMS Leigh family history researcher put out the call for "Finding Mona Budd". It resulted in a response from a member of the Smee family who owned The Grosvenor Beach Café on the South side of Chalkwell Esplanade where Mona worked before the start of the war. Heather's research even uncovered a picture of staff of the café which is believed to include Mona. Her catering skills from the Grosvenor Beach Café became invaluable when Mona joined the Pier Caterer as his assistant.

The Luftwaffe's attack on the Pier on 22nd November, 1939

Lord Haw Haw's warning on 21st October 1939 was not lost on Captain Champion. It clearly meant that the Luftwaffe would be coming to bomb Southend Pier out of existence. "The dark clouds of war are looming over us" Churchill famously declared. This was not just a metaphor. It is the winter of 1939 and the skies were truly dark and cloudy most of the time. Captain Champion declared to his senior officers that the Germans would come on the first clear night. On the morning of 22nd November just one month after the 'Germany Calling' broadcast Captain Champion went to Captain A. S. May, MVO., OBE., RN., Chief of Staff and said more or less as follows:

"I have a feeling that by all the signs tonight will be the sort of night on which they might try

something against the pier and anchorage." He instructed Captain May to "... get all the machine guns, gunners and signalman you can from Southend, London or where you will. Distribute the men among the ships. Instruct the men how to take the bearing of a 'splash' so that we can get a cross bearing fixed on any mine they drop and tell the ships to be ready for anything with everything they've got." Captain May managed to obtain 19 Lewis guns and 35 men. In small groups the men were put aboard the anchored convoy ships just before dark to watch and wait. 5 men were posted on the pier.

Captain Champion's hunch was right. At 22.00 hrs the attack began after dropping 14 parachute mines in the estuary on the way. The attack lasted for about half an hour. The ships were ready; the pier was ready. They blazed away with the guns, with rockets, with Verry's lights and everything they had. Though limited in force it was a tremendous display. One aircraft was downed and in veering off, others were hit when they ran into serious ack ack a little distance away up river at Purfleet. Captain Champion, his staff and many civilians came out onto the sea front to see the fireworks. An airman was heard to say that the show they put up was enough to frighten any air force away and to make them think "This place is much too heavily defended". Our Champion's foresight was to have incalculable consequences. The Germans never attacked the pier again. They limited themselves to dropping parachute mines in the Estuary which had devastating effect to begin with but led to intense and successful minesweeping operations.

Supplies to industries on the river continued. 60 million tons of coal a year was needed to give light and heat to homes and keep the steam trains running. The importance of coal cannot be overstated. 106,500,000 tons of shipping passed through the ports between 1939 and 1945. All of these ships had to sail past Southend Pier where they were controlled, monitored and recorded. Parliament continued to sit and the War Cabinet continued with its business.

Number One Officer on the base Lieut. Commander Sir Joseph Gurney Braithwaite 1st Baronet and an MP

Sitting MP for Sheffield Holderness and a Southend NCS officer was Lieutenant-Commander, Sir Joseph Gurney Braithwaite 1st Baronet. MP Gurney Braithwaite continued to attend the House of Commons sittings while at Southend throughout the war and relayed interesting reports for publication in Southend's NCS magazine 'Spun Yarn'. These reports were entitled "Under Big Ben" but using the pseudonym "Jimmy the One". They were just one feature in the widely read and popular Spun Yarn magazine but gave valuable insight on the workings of government in wartime. See first of these reports copied from original Edition 1 of Spun Yarn, February 1941 on P 29.

As the Naval Control Service operation in Southend grew under Captain Champion and his elite band of naval officers, the pre-war boarding houses and empty properties of absentee landlords were requisitioned for use by the NCS. Along the five miles of seafront, at its westerly end there were Nissan hut canteens in the roadway. The canteens sat 2,500 at a time with two sittings. The whole sea front was closed to the public. Access required special ID. Sadly few photographs of this enormous occupation exist as photographs were banned.

July 1940 Tragedy. Large Losses. Black Thursday. Cessation of Southend convoys across the Atlantic.

On 3rd July 1940 Convoy OA 178 assembled off Southend. It consisted of 14 merchant ships, escorted by corvette HMS Clarkia. The Convoy Commodore was Capt. R. P. Galer in SS Peterton. The convoy passed the Straits of Dover that night and was in the Channel about 20 nautical miles off Portland Bill. At 1300 hrs. on 4th July two groups of German Junkers Ju 87 Stuka dive bombers attacked the convoy. They attacked in waves of six aircraft each dropping 50kg bombs. There was no Allied air cover and the attack lasted two hours. One ship the MV Dallas City was sunk and five others badly damaged. One of these, the SS Antonio rescued 67 survivors, some with serious injuries.

A number of the ships took shelter in Portland Harbour but the bombers (stationed near Calais) attacked them again. Unfortunately, in the harbour was the anti-aircraft ship HMS Foylbank. She was badly damaged and sank next day with the loss of 176 lives. Other ships in Portland Harbour were also sunk or damaged. At dusk, those convoy ships that had remained at sea were attacked by German e.boats. Four more ships were sunk and one damaged including two Dutch and one Estonian merchantmen.

On Thursday 25th July, convoy CW8 left Southend. It consisted of 21 merchant ships. On leaving the Thames Estuary a German spotter plane was seen in the sky. This augured badly for the convoy as it now entered what had become the most bitterly contested stretch of water in the world. The Germans had arrived in Calais where there were not only Luftwaffe bases but big guns on the French coast. As the convoy passed through The Straits of Dover they suffered the full blast of heavy guns from the French mainland, followed by Stuka bomber and e.boat attacks. Out of the 21 merchant ships 11 were sunk as well as two Royal Navy destroyers.

On this occasion there was some assistance from the RAF who sent Hurricanes and Spitfires including from Hornchurch and Southend. Southend Airport was then known as Rochford Aerodrome and part of 54 Squadron. More assistance was requested but denied. Only 20 + aircraft were scrambled to meet 90 German fighters and bombers. They were greatly outnumbered and yet against impossible odds were equal to their task. On that day six brave pilots were killed and their spitfires lost. This day became known as 'Black Thursday' and it now was impossible to sail from Southend around Dover and through the Channel which had been Southend NCS route to the Atlantic. Most Atlantic convoys would now leave from Liverpool in the West.

Extract From Battle of Britain Records for 25th July 1940 (Black Thursday)

Thursday July 25th 1940
Weather:

Overnight rain periods expected to clear and give way to a fine day with only a thin layer of cloud. Still cool for the time of year but winds expected to be light. Heavier cloud was expected by evening with the possibility of rain periods.

Operations in Detail:

The weather had improved enough during the early morning for German Stuka and E-boat attacks on a convoy working its way through the Dover Straits. It was a disaster for the convoy as they were pounded by heavy guns from the French mainland as well. Eleven merchant coal ships of convoy CW8 out of twenty-one were sunk in the Straits as well as two Royal Navy destroyers. A new tactic was used by the Luftwaffe, the escorting Bf109s came in at sea level to be met by the Spitfires of 65 Squadron (Hornchurch) while the Ju87 Stuka's came out of the sky to dive bomb the convoy. 32 Squadron Biggin Hill (Hurricanes) and 615 Squadron Kenley (Hurricanes) came in to assist the sea level dogfight with fifty Bf109s. 54 Squadron Rochford (Spitfires) answered the call for assistance from the escorting naval vessels and engaged Bf109s that had arrived to assist the Ju87s. Like the previous day, 54 Squadron was to suffer badly, but

with one Spitfire to every five Bf109s, they were lucky not to lose more than three aircraft.

1430hrs, The convoy only just past Folkestone, and the Luftwaffe sent another forty Ju88's with an escort of over fifty Bf109s to make a final attack on the convoy. Although the British pilots pressed for more fighters in combat areas, their request was dismissed as command stated that " .... if we try to meet them on a one to one basis, then Fighter Command would have no fighters left after a couple of weeks." Only eight Spitfires of 64 Squadron (Kenley) were scrambled to meet the ninety German fighters and bombers, twelve Spitfires of 54 Squadron (Hornchurch) and a flight of Hurricanes from 111 Squadron (Croydon). The Hurricanes and Spitfires were vastly outnumbered by five to one, almost impossible odds, but the RAF pilots were equal to the task.

Pilot Officer D.R.Turley-George 54 Squadron RAF [1]

The 109s coming at us from above as we still struggled for height -Way* being hit and falling away out of sight [he was dead]. I remember the 109 attacking me from the port side, my trying to turn in towards him, the loud bangs of his cannon-shells striking my Spitfire as he hit me from an almost full deflection angle; and even through the pounding fear that I felt, admiring his marks-manship. A few seconds later, with my aeroplane miraculously still answering apparently normally to the controls, finding myself behind two Me 109s, aligning my sight on one, pressing the gun button - and the guns failing to fire; then diving out of the fight to return to base.'

*FIL B.H.(Wonky) Way 54 Squadron Hornchurch

After this days fighting, 54 Squadron Hornchurch was north for a brief rest They had been constantly in adion for the past three weeks, had flown in excess of 800 flying hours, had 506 operational sorties to their credit, had lost five experienced pilots and had twelve of their aircraft destroyed.

The tactic here was to meet the bombers head on at full throttle then as they dispersed they pulled upwards to meet the oncoming Bf109's. The tactic worked, and both fighters and bombers withdrew. With 64 Squadron and 111 Squadron returning to refuel, the German formation, strengthened by another staffel circled and returned to the convoy. Here they sank a further five merchantmen and seriously damaged four others. (Only 2 out of 21 were to reach their destination of Portland.)

AVM Keith Park was all in favour of attacking the bombers "head on". He maintained that they were very vulnerable from the front, very poorly armed, had very little armour protection and often flew in tight formations which meant that they had very little chance of manoeuvring for fear of hitting another bomber. "Attack the ones in front" he urged, "If you shoot them down, the formation will break up in confusion, then you can take your pick."

But such tactics could be dangerous. It called for accurate shooting and one must pull away sharply to avoid collision. ACM Hugh Dowding would not approve such tactics, it was too dangerous for our young pilots to adopt, but many brave and skillful pilots responded to Keith Parks instruction. [2]

I will say, the old Hun certainly tried hard, but they did not like that headon business. One could see the leader carrying on straight, but the followers wavering; drawing out sideways to the flanks, and in some cases just plain leaving the formation.

F/L R.M.B.D.Duke-Wooley 253 & 23 Squadrons RAF.

THE CASUALTIES: (JULY 25TH)

1455hrs: Dover. Spitfire P9451. 64 Squadron Kenley. {Lost at sea)
F/O A.J.O. Jeffrey. Killed. (Was last seen crashing into the Channel) (Body washed up on Dutch coast)

1500hrs: Off Dover. Spitfire R6707. 54 Squadron Rochford. (Lost at sea)
F/Lt B.H. "Wonky" Way. Presumed drowned. (Shot down by Bf109 and crashed into Channel)

1540hrs: Hawkinge Airfield. Spitfire R6693. 610 Squadron Biggin Hill. (Aircraft destroyed)
S/L A.T. Smith. Killed. (Crashed and burnt out after stalling on landing. Previously in combat with Bf109)

1745hrs: Off Folkestone Kent. Spitfire L1035. 64 Squadron Kenley. (Lost at sea)
Sub/Lt F.D. Paul. Died of Injuries. (Shot down by Bf109, captured by Germans but died 30.7.40

1810hrs: Dover. Spitfire R6816. 54 Squadron Rochford. (Aircraft destroyed)
P/O A. Finnie. Killed. (Hit by gunfire from Bf109 and crashed at Kingsdown, nr Dover)

2345hrs: Porthtowan Cornwall. Spitfire P9493. 234 Squadron St Eval. (Aircraft destroyed)
P/O G.K. Gout. Killed. (Crashed just outside town. Circumstances not known)

To counter the enemy threat of aircraft bombing and strafing our convoy ships we needed more than just destroyer escorts. Two new measures were introduced. DEMS and Kite Balloons. DEMS stands for Defensively Equipped Merchant Ship. DEMS Gunners might be naval or army personnel. They were trained to use mainly Lewis guns which they carried with them and when allocated a ship would board and in cramped conditions find themselves a place to secure the Lewis gun to the ship's rail and hunker down. On larger vessels they might be required to use retro fitted fixed Oerlikon cannon mainly from WW1. DEMS gunners would have to travel to Southend where their convoy ship would be allocated to them. Spun Yarn contains harrowing stories written by DEMS gunners of their experiences.

Kite Balloons had been used successfully during WW1 and now in WWII were tethered to ships in Southend by RAF personnel stationed on the Pier. The purpose of appropriately named kite balloons was to prevent aircraft from flying low over a vessel inhibiting its ability to fire and drop bombs accurately. A kite balloon would be tethered by a cable with a winch to allow adjustment of its height. On land very much larger kite balloons were known as "barrage balloons" and were used to protect cities, ports and airfields against low flying enemy aircraft. On 15th May 1940 barrage balloons in the Anchorage were struck by lightning, exploded and caught fire. In the year from May 1941 to May 1942 10,000 balloon operations were completed in the Thames with 5,222 in Southend and the remainder at Tilbury.

Portable Lewis Gun and Fixed Oerlikon for DEMS Gunners

Brexit Irony – Don't Mention the War!

It is perhaps worth reflecting at this point on a stark irony. The first six nations, of what is the European Union that we have now divorced ourselves from, were Germany, France, The Netherlands, Italy, Belgium and Luxembourg. All were dominated in the war by Germany. Italy as an ally and

France, The Netherlands, Belgium and Luxembourg were brutally subjugated under German occupation.

To extricate ourselves via Brexit we fought the will of 27 nation members of which at least 20 were occupied or dominated by Germany during WWII when Great Britain stood alone in Europe fighting a tyranny. Nobody is in any doubt that today Germany is the dominant political and economic power in the EU. What she could not achieve by the brutality of war she has achieved by more peaceful means. All credit must be given to the German people for their typical and characteristic hard work in rebuilding their country out of the ruins of war. Perhaps the final irony for Great Britain is that Germany's Chancellor, Angela Merkel, is espousing the creation of a European Army for the future. Who will dominate that I wonder? Don't mention the war!

Spun Yarn – The Journal of Thames Naval Control Southend

These journals or magazines can give only a limited insight into the day to day life of this time of great events. However, they offer the most valuable and important record, written as they happened, by the people who were involved. There were 9 editions in all of which I have complete copies.

'Spun Yarn' captures the atmosphere of NCS operations with the characteristic stiff upper lip demeanour of the British in wartime, with general news items, serious contributions from convoy commodores, humorous well written pieces, cartoons and Lieut. Commander Gurney Braithwaite MP's parliamentary reports.

The cover of the magazine shows a convoy at anchor with a Sun Tug. It is the creation of well-known marine artist, and Southend NCS member, N. Southeby Pitcher (1889 – 1959) whose marine paintings are sought after today at auction. Other well-known writers, illustrators, artists and cartoonists were on the NCS staff at Southend making the magazine popular at the time and now a valuable historical record. The only way to even partially demonstrate the rare atmosphere that surrounded the lives of those involved is to select copies of original pages from the various Spun Yarn editions just as they appeared. This may be a lengthy process but one for which I make no apology.

Throughout the war there was a saying "Careless words costs lives". It is not surprising therefore that you will often see in the pages of Spun Yarns, blanks where there should be the names of places or ships or other information.

The First Edition of Spun Yarn appeared in February 1941. At the beginning of each edition there appears a 'Roll of Honour' naming those killed in action. Below the Roll of Honour are 'Awards', 'Promotions' and those 'Mentioned in Despatches'.

It has to be remembered that paper was scarce and articles were typewritten. Copies for distribution were typed on to stencils and run off on hand operated duplicators.

Rita. Barham.

SPUN YARN

N. Sotheby Pitcher.
1940

1941   -   FEBRUARY.   -   1941

The Journal of the Thames Naval Control.

Pages 3 - 8 of the first edition is an account of Southend's great part in the evacuation from Dunkirk which took place 9 months earlier. One of the heroes, Lieut. T. M Rumbold RNVR, whose exploits you will read, rescued 700 soldiers from Dunkirk. By the time of the magazine's publication he had been killed by a mine just North of Ramsgate on 21st December 1940, as Boarding Officer on Sun Tug IX. See Page 2 'Roll of Honour'.

Pages 5, 6 and 8 are about Lieut. M. Solomon RNVR and read like something from a Boys Own adventure story. For his gargantuan efforts and harrowing experiences Solomon received the D.S.C. Lieut. Solomon's story is related by an unknown contributor but Soloman himself is quoted in his own words (second last paragraph page 8) where he extolls the virtues and courage of others whose death he witnessed.

I admit to a tear on reading this.

It is a must read as an example of the duty and comradeship that typified the British in wartime and the contribution of those serving in Thames Naval Control.

The Martin Solomon story is not in any way meant to lessen the many heroic acts of others at Dunkirk. "Operation Dynamo" as it was called led to the greatest rescue of an army in the history of warfare (330,000 men saved).

Special mention must be made of The Medway Queen which in peacetime was a paddle steamer pleasure boat, regularly taking on passengers at Southend Pier. She became known as "The Heroine of Dunkirk" for her incredible contribution to Operation Dynamo.

The Medway Queen was requisitioned in 1939 and fitted out as a minesweeper, working the Estuary waters, before being reconverted for Dunkirk passenger duties. I cannot recount the ship's many hazardous exploits here but they are well documented elsewhere and there exists today a Medway Queen Preservation Society. The Medway Queen went to Dunkirk under enemy fire 7 times. She even shot down one enemy plane. The total number of men saved and brought home by The Medway Queen was over 7,000. She then returned to minesweeping duties until demob, and after a refit, once again became a paddle steamer pleasure boat.

In about 1949 I was privileged to go on a school trip from Bournemouth Park Junior school on the Medway Queen up the Medway to Rochester. I well remember that we had to write an essay about the trip on which I was complimented. Little did we know at the time of Heroine of Dunkirk's history.

Even in those dark days of 1940, recorded in Spun Yarn's first edition, spirits were kept up with typical stiff-upper-lip British humour. On page 14 there is a well written humorous rhyme in good meter entitled "Alas A Lass".

Here on pages 21 - 22 is the first of Gurney Braithwaite MP's "Beneath Big Ben" reports on his attendance at The House of Commons having travelled from the Southend Base.

Next I include a ditty by A. W. Prentice (Chief Yeoman Signals) entitled "Ten Little Messerschmitts". Sung to the tune of 'Ten Green Bottles'. See the last line which is the best.

It was on 18th June 1940 in the House of Commons
that Churchill made that most inspiring speech –

"Let us therefore brace ourselves to our duty and so bear ourselves that if the British Commonwealth and Empire lasts for a thousand years men will say,

This was their finest hour".

ROLL · of · HONOUR

Vice Admiral G. B. Washington, C.M.G.
Vice Admiral H. Hill Smith, D.S.O.
Rear Admiral E. J. C. Mackinnon.
Rear Admiral J. C. Hamilton.
Lieut. T. M. Rumbold, R.N.V.R.
Ord. Sig. Harold Porter, C/JX 172588.
Ord. Sig. J. Turner, C/JX 172980
Ord. Sig. Walter Poole, C/JX 174064.

NEW ~ YEAR HONOURS

O.B.E.

Commander R. G. Thelwell, R.D., R.N.R.

GEORGE MEDAL.

Lieut. Commander C. H. Poulton, R.N.

MEDAL OF THE ORDER OF THE BRITISH EMPIRE.

C.Y.S. R. F. Barrington.
C.P.O.Tel. H. G. Miller.

MENTIONED IN DESPATCHES.

Commander D. M. B. Baker, R.D., R.N.R.
P. O. Tel. S. S. Maynard.
Convoy Ldg. Sig. R. F. Bennett.
Convoy Ldg. Sig. C. A. Day.
Convoy Ldg. Sig. C. M. Hearn.
Convoy Ldg. Sig. B. B. Hills.
Ldg. Sig. H. S. Nottage, R.N.V.R.
Convoy Sig. J. H. L. Sulman.

CONGRATULATIONS

To the following on being promoted to the rank of Tempy.Sub.Lt.

Sig. J. W. Mackintosh.
Sig. G. F. Howe.
Sig. J. H. L. Sulman.
Sig. R. Townshend.
Convoy. Sig. R. G. Sheffield.
Convoy. O. Sig. R. W. Stevens.
Convoy. O. Sig. R. M. Dixon Spain.

".... The ready willingness with which seamen from every walk of
life came forward to assist their brother seamen of the Royal Navy
will not readily be forgotten.

Their Lordships also realise that success was only rendered possible by the great effort made by all shore establishments........"

(From the Admiralty Message of congratulation to the Fighting Services)

The Dunkirk zero hour struck, for Southend, a little after 2 a.m.
on the 27th May, when instructions were received from the Admiralty to
search the coast for small craft suitable for transporting troops from
shore to ship.

Southend was not the only Base which was asked to do this, but
the Admiralty were particularly keen to get as many of what they called
"Southend Tiddlers" for the very difficult work off the Dunkirk Beaches.
The N.C.S. London and Gravesend were also called upon to do their share
and as soon as day broke, officers were out in all directions searching
and making contact with Owners of suitable craft. In the River Crouch
quite a few were found. From the mouth of the Thames right up as far
as Teddington a stream of pleasure and passenger craft of all shapes and
sizes began the trickle - ever increasing until it reached a flood;
while Southend Pierhead and Sheerness Dockyard were kept on their toes
for days, coping with requirements, handing out iron rations, kitting
up, equipping and arming the crews of the rescue craft who were destined
to play so glorious a part in the epic events of the succeeding days.

In London, the N.C.S. Boarding Officers scoured the River for more
and more vessels, and over the telephone line from Gravesend came a
never ceasing stream of reports on movements. At Southend, Commander
Boles, assisted by Lieut. Comdr. Jeyes, R.N.R., Lieut. G. Norton, R.N.V.R.
Paym. Lieut. C. Millson, R.N.R., Lieut. C. Wright, R.N.V.R. and Lieut.
T.M.Rumbold, R.N.V.R. amongst others, searched every yard and creek from
Burnham to Benfleet for motor cruisers, bawleys and cockle boats, indeed
for any form of self-propelling craft which were not too deep in draft
and were able to make the journey across the Channel. And here let it
be recorded to their honour, that the owners, without exception, gave
these craft willingly. Great was the disappointment of those whose
boats did not satisfy the requirements of the Navy. Many of the owners
were working fishermen and their boats represented their livelihood, yet
they gave them readily, content, if need be to give their lives as well
if by so doing their brothers across the water could be extricated from
dire peril.

- 3 -

Indeed for those whose privilege it was to organise and to marshal those forces in their work of rescue, the keenness and the anxiety to be of service of the fishermen and yachtsmen of Burnham, Southend, Leigh and Benfleet could not but arouse the deepest admiration, with a realisation that the spirit of Elizabeth's England was again at work among us!

And so for four or five hectic days and nights the Naval Bases on the Thames searched for and found and equipped a motley fleet of craft running into hundreds, manned in a large number of cases by their owners and supported by selected Naval Officers and Ratings.

It would need volumes to describe in detail the adventures of those who sailed forth on the coast enterprise. Some were dogged by the worst luck and never succeeded in reaching their destination. The "NEW PRINCE OF WALES" for instance, broke down before she reached The Downs. The Tug "SUN V" (Lieut. Beresford Wright, R.N.V.R.) was run down and badly damaged in the mist by a destroyer also hurrying to the work of rescue. The "RENOWN" being towed by a Trawler fell a victim to German mines, and her crew (three civilians) - all Southend fishermen, perished gloriously for England. Many of the boats sent from the Thames never returned. Some were beached on the French coast, their crews having performed prodigies in ferrying the Army to the safety of the larger craft. Others were sunk by enemy action or through the hazards of the sea. All gave a good account of themselves and worthily upheld the traditions of their fathers.

A volume could be filled in recounting the incidents which occurred in the adventures experienced by individuals during these great days. Lieut. C. Wright, R.N.V.R. with Lieut. G. Norton, R.N.V.R., experienced the most exciting adventures in the "FOSSA" and "SOUTHEND BRITANNIA" when in charge of a flotilla of 8 - 10 motor-boats. The story of their efforts and their disappointments due to break-down of machinery or over-strain of craft designed for quite other purposes makes most interesting reading. Yet with all their rough luck this flotilla succeeded in rescueing many brave fellows from the beaches of Dunkirk, and on one occasion picked up a derelict raft in the Downs full of British soldiers, and towed them successfully into Ramsgate.

Lieut. T. M. Rumbold, R.N.V.R., in the motor-boat "VIKING" was able to reach the beach at La Panne in the early morning of the 29th., and proceeded to ferry troops from the beaches to the ships until fuel became so low that he was forced to give up and return, but seven hundred British soldiers owe their safety to the "VIKING" and her dauntless crew. She returned again, but appears to have been shelled by the Germans, and her engines damaged so that the good work of the previous day could not be repeated.

- 4 -

24

To record adequately the adventures of Lieut. M. Solomon, R.N.V.R. who richly deserved the D.S.C. which rewarded his exploits, would fill the whole of this Number. At one stage his craft was subject to severe air attack by approximately 20 enemy aircraft, bombs falling as near as 15 yards from the ships, so that his little convoy had to break formation. However, three or four Spitfires drove off the enemy, and seven 'planes crashed into the sea. Then they reached the beaches, and found themselves subject to heavy bombardment from the Shore. However, eventually they reached Dunkirk itself and succeeded in getting on board about two hundred men from the Mole and transferred them to other ships returning to Ramsgate.

To and from they went into Dunkirk Harbour and out again to the waiting ships. They picked up, among others, two German prisoners who were attempting to get to England, and finally they proceeded to Ramsgate laden with soldiers of the First Division, including the Colonel of the Worcesters and Officers of the Camerons.

Arriving at Ramsgate, Lieut. Solomon surveyed the damage to his craft. The "RENOWN" had been sunk off Dunkirk, and all hands were lost. Fortunately, thirty or forty soldiers had just been transferred from her to a Trawler otherwise the loss would have been much greater. The "LETITIA", which was being towed by a Trawler ahead of "RENOWN" was fortunately undamaged. The total number of troops transferred to Ramsgate by the Bawley boats was over six hundred.

At the end of this good work Lieut. Solomon decided that his Bawley boats were in no condition for further service, and ordered them to return to Southend. For himself, he then obtained permission to commandeer any of the available craft in Ramsgate Harbour, and so found himself again en route for Dunkirk with the Tug "FOSSA" and the Motorboat "THERUNE", which he manned with one Petty Officer and two Sea Scouts. It was impossible at this stage to take the "FOSSA" into Dunkirk, and so he went in in the "THERUNE" alongside the Mole with the intention of ferrying troops outside to "FOSSA". As he came alongside he overheard a Naval Officer on the Mole cry "Isn't there anyone here who can deal with these Frenchmen?" Solomon is a linguist, and at once offered his services as Liaison Officer, leaving the Petty Officer in charge of the "THERUNE" to continue loading the "FOSSA", until at last three hundred men had been embarked. From then on, as he modestly put it, "due to a fair knowledge of the French language, I was able to render a certain amount of assistance to the Officer-in-Charge of the Jetty", and when as it appears, the large congestion of French troops had been got away, understanding that the Destroyer "WINCHELSEA" was the last ship to be leaving, he returned to Dover in her.

- 5 -

Solomon seems to have kept his eyes open while in Dunkirk for on return to Dover he was able to submit to the Authorities a chart giving the situation at Dunkirk with considerable detail, and this seems to have enabled him to obtain permission to again return to do what he could in assisting the further evacuation of French troops.   In this case he went with an Advance Party in two R.A.F. Motor-boats with two French Officers and two Naval Officers, all under Commander Cluston. The boat in which Solomon was travelling, however, never reached her destination.   They were attacked by four enemy aircraft, bombed and sunk instantaneously, but marvellous to relate no casualties seem to have been sustained, except in the case of Solomon who was wounded in the right leg by the explosion.   The aircraft then proceeded to machine-gun the swimmers   in the water, but apparently unsuccessfully.   Commander Cluston shouted to the remaining R.A.F. boat not to risk being bombed, but to proceed   to Dunkirk, while he and his companions clinging to the wreck decided   to wait rescue from other craft.   At this stage a French Officer said that he had seen an empty boat about six miles off, and Solomon asked permission to see if he could swim towards her so as to bring her back.   By this time the water was somewhat choppy, so that it was impossible for Solomon to see the boat he was after, and he only caught occasional glimpses of the shore.   Three and a half hours later at 2230 he appears to have sighted a Destroyer's cutter, which however, was too high out of the water for him to board her as by this time he was bordering on exhaustion.   Before finally deciding to swim for the German shore, however, he fortunately swam around the boat and found a fender hanging down the other side and with the aid of this and using the remains of his kit as a ladder, he was able to get aboard.   He then lashed the helm hard over, and then attempted to row the cutter with one oar in the direction in which he imagined the survivors to be, but the time was   approaching midnight and even Solomon's irrepressible exuberance was forced to face the facts.   It was dark.   The cutter was far too large and heavy for him to manage in his exhausted state.   The distance was far too great, and he had been trying for over an hour with little effect to move her in the direction in which he wished to go.   It seemed that only capture by the Germans lay before him, so that nothing remained for him but to destroy all personal belongings and identifications, and to   throw overboard what remained of his kit to prevent being identified by the enemy. His dismay may be imagined when an hour and a half later he was passed by a British Destroyer but twenty-five yards away, but was unable to attract their attention by his shouts.   At last a fishing boat, the "STELLA MAVIS" came by, and Solomon shouted alternately in French and English, until he was finally picked up and taken aboard.   Here he was given a much needed refresher in the shape of Vin Ordinaire, and dressed in French sailor's uniform he was put into a bunk where suffering from complete exhaustion he apparently passed out for a while.   But not for very long, for an hour later found him persuading the French skipper to alter his course to Dover instead of trying to reach Dunkirk in daylight

- 6 -

A WAR DRAWING BY A REAL" WAR-ARTIST" !!!

this drawing is from an original by one of Southends
Dunkirk Heroes—

the Editors—

- 7 -

where he was certain of destruction. For five hours he helped him to navigate towards Dover. Not long after day-break they were run down by a Torpedo-boat, but fortunately were not badly damaged and managed to make Dover Harbour safely. But even there the adventure was not at an end for the Commanding Officer of the French Escort vessel suspected Solomon of being a spy, saying "Il pretend être Anglais, mais moi je crois qui'il est Allemand parcequ'il parle le Francais trop bien". Nothing daunted Solomon persuaded the Frenchman to put him ashore so that he might be arrested by the British Authorities. Rather naively his story ends "1030 successfully arrested by a Naval Lieutenant Commander and reported to Commander Goodenough and Admiral Ramsay".

Unfortunately we have not a photo of Lieut. Solomon in his fisherman's get-up. Even his apparently iron constitution could not entirely ignore the night's experiences, and he was sent to Chatham Hospital in an ambulance where his wounds were healed and he had a much deserved and needed rest.

Of the companions who were bombed with Solomon in the R.A.F. boat only one - an R.A.F. mechanic - survived. While clinging to the remains of the motor-boat, he was picked up by a Destroyer. According to him, the rest had already died from exposure.

"Although I realise," wrote Solomon, "that it is of no consolation to those bereaved, I feel that the extraordinary courage of all the poor fellows in the water should be recorded. Even though they must have known that the end was near, they never grumbled nor were they afraid; they even went so far as to ask permission of Commander Cluston before removing their tin hats. When I left them clinging around the wreck, although already suffering from exposure, they were singing and discussing old times together. Commander Cluston's courage must have helped them all as it helped me. Although exhausted himself, he continued to chat, encourage and white-lie to the end".

These were typical of the many English men who in those fateful days set out to rescue their fellow Englishmen and French allies from the clutches of a relentless foe. Whether they were Navy, Army or Air Force or volunteer civilian crews and Thames fishermen, they all helped to snatch victory from the jaws of defeat.

"THEIR FAME LIVETH FOR EVERMORE".

Alas A lass!

Sing a song of sorrow for the charming little "Wren"
Who comes to serve her country, armed with powder puff and pen.
Who comes to brighten working hours of sailors on the shore,
With her feminine attraction or? (Just that and nothing more).
Now, the chief of all the Wrens, obeying some vile spinster urge,
Was dressing all the little Wrens in yards of Pusser's serge.
The poor girls were despondent, and said they all would feel
That, wrapped in hairy jumpers, they would lose their sex appeal.
These dull black shoes and stockings would never, never please;
And what's the use of skirts that hang two feet below the knees?
A collar with two rolls of tape won't draw caressing arms,
Unless it's old "Three Badge Men" (who understand such charms).
We are sure a flannel dicky or a little cotton vest
Will just produce a tickle and a cold upon the chest.
A lanyard hung around the neck is almost bound to slip.
A black silk hasn't any use except to "Darken ship".
We hear the big white chief of Wrens may yet unbend a bit
And issue all with "tailor mades", a style that will be fit
To serve one's King and Country in - and keep one's self respect,
To play the game as Churchill and Lord Nelson would expect.
We always must remember that a charming little "Wren"
Likes to look attractive every now and then,
And sailor men still realise, as they toss upon the brine,
That "camis" never were made up to uniform design".

- 14 -

BENEATH BIG BEN

by
" TIMMY THE ONE "

A war-time Parliament must, of necessity, form a striking contrast to its peace-time prototype. For one thing, the greater issue of national survival swallows up much domestic controversy and party strife, while an all-party Government embracing all shades of political thought sits all-powerful without any organised opposition worthy of the name.

In its way this is not a good thing, as nothing keeps Ministers up to the mark more effectively than an alert and efficient opposition, able and willing to replace them. But the British Parliament is a flexible institution well suited by tradition to reflect the mood of the people, so to-day the Churchill Government, while enjoying unanimous support in the vital objective of winning the war, finds itself subjected to a hundred criticisms on points of detail and administration.

For one thing, there are rather more than a hundred Members serving in the Forces who are vocal on service matters. There are some who say that this is a bad thing, as no man can serve two masters. But M.Ps in uniform are, in fact, serving one master - the State - and it would be an odd and contemptible House of Commons which voted the country into war while its able-bodied members sat back and took no active part in the conflict.

The present Parliament should have come to an end in November 1940 but its life has been prolonged by statute as a General Election in war-time is neither desirable nor practical. Millions of electors evacuated from their homes, the expense and difficulty of compiling a voting register in such circumstances, and the impossibility of holding coherent political meetings in the black-out all combine to rule out such a proposal. In many ways this is a pity as a Parliament freshly elected would be a better vehicle of public opinion than the present House which has been sitting since 1935. However, the situation is not what it seems as owing to death and retirement, the representation of some 150 constituencies has changed hands during the past five years - indeed six Ministers have come to the House during that time, so that new blood is constantly being infused.

The other day a new session was opened with all the traditional ceremonial which has grown up through the centuries. It was, however, a state opening in battle dress - gone were the royal robes and crown, gone the jewels and coronets - in their place were the garments of war with His Majesty paying to the Senior Service the compliment of appearing in naval uniform. Instead of his ancient crown he wore an Admiral's cap when reading the speech from the throne - thus symbolising his leadership of a nation on active service.

The King's speech always gives an opportunity for the House to debate "the state of the nation", and this was a worthy successor of previous occasions, with a note of healthy criticism lest Ministers should show themselves less determined than the rank and file. The address of thanks to His Majesty was moved by a Conservative, Squadron Leader Grant Ferris, Member for North St. Pancras, who has taken our Spitfires into action over the Thames Estuary on many occasions and will do so again. He spoke with enthusiasm and determination of the day when we shall dominate the air and let loose upon the enemy a British Blitzkrieg of awful intensity. The Seconder was the prosaic but very sincere Socialist member for Poplar, Mr. Key, late Mayor of the Borough which has suffered perhaps more than any from enemy action. He spoke quietly of the courage and determination of his cockney constituency voicing the unbending will of the people of London to stick it out to the end, and paying a well deserved tribute to the work of nurses, fire services and air raid wardens in the stricken area.

The subsequent debate brought criticism of such matters as the mobilisation of labour and financing of the war, while more than one Member pointed to the need for new methods of countering the serious effects of the enemy's submarine campaign in the Western Approaches to our island.

At the end of the discussion came one of those incidents which puzzle those who do not understand our institutions. Mr. McGovern, I.L.P. Member for Shettleston, moved an amendment on behalf of the small Clydeside group advocating an immediate peace conference, and condemning the continuation of the war. In almost every other belligerent country these gentlemen would have been marched off to the nearest concentration camp, but they were allowed to have their say and at the end their proposal was defeated by 341 votes to 4 - not four just men, but just four men! Thus is freedom of speech preserved amidst the sound of the guns.

Anyhow, the new session is now launched in an atmosphere of quiet confidence and grim resolve, and the House will now go on to deal with such matters as compensation for air raid damage and the problem of financing the railways.

- 22 -

TEN LITTLE MESSERSCHMITTS

Ten little Messerschmitts flying in a line,
One met a Hurricane, then there were nine.

Nine little Messerschmitts on a job of hate,
Ran into Ack Ack, then there were eight.

Eight little Messerschmitts zooming down from heaven,
One hit a Barrage Balloon, then there were seven.

Seven little Messerschmitts trying out their tricks;
One got a knock out, then there were six.

Six little Messerschmitts forced into a dive,
Up popped a Home Guard, then there were five.

Five little Messerschmitts feeling somewhat sore,
Swooped on a trawler, then there were four.

Four little Messerschmitts heading out to sea,
One met a Hudson, then there were three.

Three little Messerschmitts racing o'er the blue,
Swerved on a Destroyer, then there were two.

Two little Messerschmitts each complete with Hun,
Had a collision, then there was one.

One little Messerschmitt flying o'er Southend,
Tried it on a Convoy and that was the end.

No little Messerschmitts, poor Joe Goebbels learned,
Then -! Haw-Haw said "All ours returned".

A. W. PRENTICE, C.Y.S.

1941 ★ JUNE. ★ 1941
The Journal of the Thames Naval Control.

Pages 3 - 7 are well written graphic accounts by an unnamed signalman of his first 9 months on East Coast Convoy Duties. From being bombed on his maiden voyage followed by other disasters involving much loss of life these pages are worth reading. They typify what was experienced by many on these dangerous convoy sailings. However, undaunted by these events our signalman comes through and recounts examples of the humour and camaraderie of his shipmates. This was the hallmark of (forgive the pun) 'everybody being in the same boat'.

Page 8 features the NCS association with Southend's oldest yacht club The Alexandra Yacht Club close by. Officers from the base were made to be very welcome and many functions were held for them at the Yacht Club. Please also read bottom of the page "THE SHORT STORY" which is very funny.

Page 26 is a typical example of humour, personalised with officers' names and in rhyme.

CONVOY SIGNALMAN

I came to Southend in June 1940, an extremely raw signalman from "Royal Arthur", that home of **clerks** and artisans transformed overnight into hardy shellbacks, or so **we hoped.** The eighteen co-newcomers as well as myself were straightway **transformed** back to clerks and artisans by the dulcet tones of the M.A., **who** informed us that we were in the Navy proper now. I was badly **crushed, being** the recipient of some of his choice remarks. However, **we soon settled** down and looked eagerly forward to the day when we would **sail** on our first convoy, which was not long delayed, for one by one we became attached to a staff and proudly packed our little attache cases, entrained on the pier (first class only) and sailed. I remember that I imagined all sorts of grand actions and heroic deeds being performed by yours truly, but the sea was flat calm, the ship was a filthy Tyneside collier and we never saw a thing. However, I made up for that disappointment **by later** experiencing over a dozen bombing attacks, not to mention E-boat attacks, mines, aerial torpedoes and a couple of collisions.

That well-known character Ralph Lancaster was my schoolmaster on this trip, and fellow signalmen can imagine the superior look of a seasoned seadog that his thin face wore every time I made a faux pas. I arrived back at the Base tired and dirty, with a chest like a cockerel and a pronounced roll, notwithstanding the fact that the sea was like a sago pudding.

A word about the Merchant Navy here would not be amiss. These brave fellows, in my opinion, are doing as fine a job of work as the servicemen. Pay and conditions are notoriously bad in British ships, and the sea normally contains enough perils for the unwary. Now they are exposed to the full force of the hun attack. "If it isn't one b....... thing it's another," as one skipper remarked to me. Yet Britain still runs her shipping, even under the guns that are now mounted on the French coast. Anyone serving with these hard bitten heroes speedily realizes what a hopeless task the Jerry has to completely blockade our island. While there are ships there will be no lack of men to man them, survivors invariably want to go straight back to sea again. Spare a thought, you

- 3 -

politicians planning our New Deal for the Merchant Seamen, let them never have to struggle along under the old pre-war standards.

For us signalmen, I think that the days following the French collapse were the saddest. Crew after crew went out and caught a packet. Channel convoys became a really hazardous adventure, but no one shirked and all took their turn to run the gauntlet. Yes, those were sad days. Several fine chaps were lost and more injured and when the First Lieut. said 'off caps' at divisions we all felt a heavy feeling and dwelt for a moment on old so and so. Do you remember how we knocked back those pints at the Monument, Newcastle, or those couple of nice girls we took home after that dance at the Oxford? Only a moment's pause before we went about our duties again, but I for one retain memories of real gentlemen who have given their lives for their country.

The first time I was heavily bombed was on the maiden voyage of one of our largest colliers. I was in the saloon at the time eating dinner, when there was a terrific explosion. The skipper and second mate shot out of the door and I followed, hastily munching the remains of my sausage and mash. Explosion followed explosion, and machine gun fire seemed to be coming from all directions. Halfway up the bridge ladder I was drenched by the spray from a near miss. Dessert would have to wait, this is real action, thought I. All I did though, was to drop flat every time I heard a bomb scream. It was a high level attack and the blighters were aiming for our gleaming new white hatch covers. Although a large number of bombs fell around, we suffered little damage beyond burst steam pipes. On another occasion, I was in the middle of a signal to the Escort when from the corner of my eye I espied many Junkers 88 dive-bombers. I hoisted the alarm and stood by for the fun. They made for us, the largest ship in the convoy, and started on a dive. The Escort ran alongside and held his fire until the first rank were pulling out from the dive, and then up shot a barrage that must have made the Jerries think they had reached hell already. Two crashed and three more were severely damaged and probably destroyed, the rest fled for home as fighters appeared in the distance. The bombs missed us, but the gallant Escort was hit. I must confess that if anything had happened I would have been more of a liability than an asset for I stood on the bridge cheering as though I were at a football match, and wearing neither tin hat nor lifebelt, for which, I might add, I was suitably ticked off by the Commodore. Just one more spot of bother before we pass on. We were going along very peaceably on a bright, crisp morning. I had just finished my watch and gone below and was engaged in writing to my fiancee telling her how pleasant everything was (you know what lovers are). Suddenly there was a really pipping explosion which hurled me to the deck, and bits of plaster showered over me. Leaping up I pulled at the door, but it was jammed. It did not remain so for long, I soon showed it who was master. I made my way rapidly to the bridge and found Frankie Burnett, my oppo, dazed and damped. A dive bomber coming out of the sun had caught us unawares and laid an egg a few yards off our starboard beam, drenching the ship, including the bridge, with spray. A

- 4 -

very near miss indeed. Circling, he came again, getting into position for another try and machine-gunning, to which of course, we replied. Three times he tried a dive and then we hit him. He slipped away, skimming along the top of the waves, jettisoning his cargo en route. The Escort informed us that he subsequently crashed and that there were no survivors. I must say that these particular chaps were very brave. They pressed home the attack and fully intended that one of us should go.

Of course we are gradually getting the measure of these air attacks and are finding new weapons to combat them. Although many of our ships have been sunk, the Luftwaffe are not without their casualties, and when you read in your Evening News that H.M.S.............. has brought down a bomber in the North Sea, that is another point to us. And as we, the Convoy runners know, these points are steadily increasing.

U-Boats are another menace to our shipping. These cheery little fellows have several ways of attack. They sometimes lie becalmed in the troughs of the waves, waiting for you, or else they come up with a rush and a roar and when you open fire, dash off just as quickly. They are very partial to calm, moonless nights, when they can get amongst the merchantmen unobserved. They are very vulnerable to machine gun fire, but are difficult to hit, owing to their high speed. I remember one attack when they were preceded by aeroplanes dropping flares to assist in locating us. A night action is totally different from one in the daytime. It is very difficult to make out what is going on. Gun flashes illuminate the sea for a moment before leaving everything blacker than ever. When in convoy navigation is extremely difficult and the risk of collision very prominent. Glowing accounts cannot be written about these attacks as you really know little about them unless, of course, you are hit by a torpedo. I generally spend my time on the bridge lamenting my nice warm bunk, for of course, everybody is on duty at those times. Signalling at night is no mean task, I have been mistaken for a cat many times, and have strained my eyes trying to catch an illusive little light that keeps winking at me from the blackness. Incidentally, lack of sleep, is in my opinion, the greatest strain in this work. I once went fifty six hours without turning in, and I expect many of my chums have gone greater periods. Sometimes the bunks are not too good. I landed once bitten all over by bugs and on another occasion there was nowhere to lie down except upon the hatch covers. The navigation and manning of the ships are generally very good but on one occasion on a little coaster (which was subsequently lost with all hands) I was left at the wheel for an hour or so alone on the bridge at 0200. The first mate had the wheel as they were short-handed, and I offered to let him go below for a few minutes for a smoke. Time went by and I grew really anxious, but could not do anything but steer the course and hope for the best. When he came back it transpired that he had fallen asleep across the saloon table. So you see we have to know other things besides signalling.

- 5 -

I once, only once, mark you, caught a Commodore out on his course reckoning. But that story must keep, no names, no pack drill. Don't we know these Commodores, eh! boys? All their little idiosyncrasies; one of them takes his golf clubs with him (he is the best of fellows) while another takes his walking stick, which incidentally dropped in the drink the other day. I must not become a budding Walter Winchell though, as I might come back to Southend and then where would I be? Nevertheless, I would like to add that I personally, have received fine treatment from these important bigwigs; they have treated me more like a fellow warrior than an ordinary rating.

Mines are another insidious weapon which the men who go down to the sea in ships have to face. I have never myself been in a ship that has blown up, but several of the fellows at the Base have. It is nerve-racking because of its unexpectedness; there is no warning and it generally seems to happen at the most annoying moments such as at meal times, or when one has just gone below after completing a four hour watch. The most terrible sight that I have seen was a tanker that blew up and burst into flames. It is a horrible thing to behold a gallant ship ablaze from stem to stern, with loud explosions racking her tortured hull internally. She blazed for days, burning down to the water's edge.

Among this chronicle of excitement you may think that there is little humour, but you would be wrong, for since I joined up I have had more laughs than in five years of civvy life. My comrades are, in between times, the gayest and merriest bunch that one could wish to meet. I have literally dozens of anecdotes of happy hours and escapades from various ports. If anybody knows how to enjoy themselves ashore, it is a sailor, for the hard knocks the sea deals out, especially in wartime, teaches one a sense of values and gives a large fund of humour and jollity.

Once we were running through the Straits of Dover in a collier, when an incident occurred which caused me much mirth, but was not so funny for the other party. The journey down was all right apart from a little shelling and the weather. This latter was atrocious, blowing a gale, snow and sleet, and everything was really dirty. I was very thankful for my duffel coat and seaboots. Coming back we ran into a thick fog, and were forced to anchor. My opposite number was "Wee" Georgie Lloyd, a lad fra' Lancashire, who had been mined on his previous trip, so naturally was a little wary. We lay opposite the German guns ensconsed at Calais. I was on the bridge with the mate when I heard a ship coming up. She loomed out of the fog and then rammed us in the starboard bow. We heeled over at an acute angle. The mate dashed below to see the damage. I jammed my legs against a post to keep upright, sounded the siren with one hand, and shone the beam of my Aldis on the hole, with the other. George, in the saloon reading, was shot on the floor by the impact. He made for the door, and on coming out on deck could hear rushing water (from the burst water tanks). The first I saw of him was a little whitefaced apparition

- 6 -

with two life jackets on, tugging at the lifebelt hanging on the side of
the bridge.   It struck me as being very funny.   I would like to add
though, that seeing I had no belt he straightway went below and fetched
one for me.

Such incidents are legion;   when the lads get together, many's the
yarn told over a pint.   Most of us are around twenty-one, but some are
only nineteen, and between us we could fill volumes with stories both hum-
ourous and gay.   When ashore, we are under the eagle eye of "Alfie" and
"Barrie" two chief yeomen, and go to instructions. Much of the credit of
our efficiency must be attributed to these two old shellbacks who are always seeking to instil more knowledge into our thick skulls.

Six of the gang were mentioned in dispatches this Christmas, notably Charlie Hearne, a most popular and cheerful chap who was unfortunately
lost at sea without knowing of the honour.   These awards show us that our
work is appreciated, and reflect very well on the general efficiency and
good conduct of the sea-going staff at the Base.   Anyone, who at this
period of the war is feeling downhearted, can think of our very small part
in this conflict, and then dwell on the navy as a whole. The recent overwhelming sea victory over the Italians in the Mediterranean should dispel
any fears of defeat that might exist.   The navy is in great spirit and
is stronger than ever.

I have not mentioned seasickness, or dwelt on the weather.   The
elements are equally as deadly as Hitler's minions, and give just as much
trouble to us.   I remember when I was in a small coaster, being very badly battered about by a real North Sea storm.   The bridge was under water
most of the time and it was impossible to remain on deck. Our boats were
damaged and everything movable on deck was carried away. The Escort sent
us a signal reading "I will lend you a couple of torpedo tubes and you can
become a submarine."   Every time she dipped and the water crashed over
the bridge, I thought we were finished, but eventually we staggered into
port looking very bedraggled. Mal de mer, to give it its posh name, is
a very deadly and horrible thing that causes intense depression and makes
one feel extremely ill.   One does not always get used to it either.   I
have seen most of the ship's company feeling squeamish, including the Captain who had been at sea thirty one years.   Needless to say I have had my
share of having to rush to the gunwhale quickly!

As I am now at Chatham for a short while, I am able to view my nine
months of East Coast work in a detached way, and if the personal pronoun
has been much in evidence in this article, it is because I was asked to
write my story; but these events can be multiplied scores of times by my
fellow shipmates engaged on convoy work.   Just think of us when next you
grumble at your butter ration, and be thankful that you don't have to
fetch it.

- 7 -

THE ALEXANDRA YACHT CLUB.

A definite feature of Naval life at Southend is the Alexandra Yacht Club, which has opened its hospitable doors to all Naval and Military Officers whose duties have brought them to Southend.

The genial Commodore, Mr. Rumsey and his Flag Officers have now become our firm friends, and one is always assured of a cheery welcome when one enters the Club. Amongst many others, one may mention Mr. Charles Parsons, Mr. Alfred Dean, Doctor Derry, Mr. Earl, Mr. Groves, Doctor Bewes and also the Secretary, Mr. Warren. Last, but by no means least, comes "Harry" the Steward, who, with his never failing source of Irish humour, charms one even when the bombs are falling in the mud.

The Club has been the scene of not a few Service celebrations during the past months. A very pleasant cocktail party was given by the 69th Battery, Heavy A/A Royal Artillery on 16th March, to which the Navy were invited, and which was followed by a Snooker Match between Army and Navy, and wound up by community singing in which the Colonel and Captain Meikle, R.N.R., contributed their full quota.

Officers promoted, or on being appointed elsewhere are in the habit of celebrating or making their farewells to their fellow officers in the Club, and the hospitality of its members is a source of never failing appreciation to us.

On Captain Meikle's recent departure, the opportunity was taken to present to the Club from the Officers of the Thames Naval Control, a small replica of a convoy Commodore's Pendant, which now hangs proudly in its place. May it do so for many years in remembrance of the good comradeship of these hazardous days.

THE SHORT STORY

by

John Scott Hughes, Lieut. R.N.V.R.

Some maintain that the short story is a most difficult thing to write. It isn't really. The difficult thing is to write a good short story. Once I heard some people talking about the short story. At length they became pretty well unanimous that the short story must fail unless it contained religion, humour, high society, action and sex. At which point one of the party remarked, "I have it, how about this" -

"My God," laughed the Duchess, "let go my leg!"

- 8 -

The perfect Commodore, they say
is one whose convoy's underway
exactly at the time it should
but this of course is understood
indeed, he always reaches port
precisely at the hour he ort,
this would be easy it would seem
but there are obstacles between
which he must do his best to shun
namely the traps laid by the Hun
torpedo, bomb and gun and mine
are things which he must see in time
his Escorts are so dear to him
that it would be a major sin
if signals sent to them were terse
they should be flashed in gentle verse
Lester Newman (with the beard)
fills this bill so I have heard.

                          A N O N.

FROM THE COMMODORE TO H.M.S. VIVIEN.......

"We have beaten the programme and slipped by the Hun,
    It is hardly a sham to have a good run,
With such weather and you to see us all thro'
    From Nore to the Forth - so long, thanks to you."

THE REPLY FROM H.M.S. VIVIEN........

"Your signal dear Newman, I think
    Calls, in near future, for drink,
The toast I suggest is to you as the best
May you always be saved if you sink!"

There was a B.O. with a beard,
Who said, "It is just as I feared,
    Two A.T.S. and a W.R.E.N.
    A W.A.A.F. and a H.E.N.
Have all made a nest in my beard.

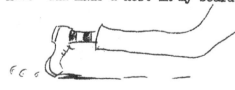

The Chief of the Sick Bay is Cumber
Whose motto is "Duty, not Slumber".
    To people with ills,
    He administers pills,
He is feared from the Thames to the Humber.

- 26 -

1941 ★ OCTOBER. ★ 1941

The Journal of the Thames Naval Control.

Page 2 Roll of Honour includes MBEs and OBEs for Sun Tug Dunkirk duties. Also see note of presentation to Sub. Lieut. H. Downs by the Royal Humane Society of a Testimonial on Vellum for saving the life of a ship's Master.

Pages numbered 3 - 5 with the heading "Southend buys a Destroyer" relate to fund raising during War Weapons Week in which Southend collected a total of £524,833 (equivalent of just under £29 million today) from a series of organised events. This enormous sum was given to The Treasury by NCS Southend for the purchase of a destroyer. In between pages 3 and 5 are two pages of photographs from the Southend Standard 12th July edition. Among others they feature a picture of A. V. Alexander, First Lord of the Admiralty giving an opening speech at the start of War Weapons Week.

On the second page of photographs there is an ancient wooden stock anchor standing outside Capt. Champion's office at No. 8 Royal Terrace. That anchor now has a special place in full view on entering the grounds of 'Porters' the Mayor of Southend's official residence.

Pages 21 & 22 are a special "Beneath Big Ben" by Gurney Braithwaite, MP. It recalls a speech by Churchill to the The House on returning from a U.S. visit to see President Roosevelt. Of special interest to Southend was the account on the second page where our A. P. Herbert as MP presided over a private members meeting at which Gurney Braithwaite attended. AP presided over Admiral of the Fleet, Sir Roger Keyes, Admiral Sir Percy Royds, Rear Admiral Beamish, Lord Winterton, Viscount Astor and others. The importance of AP as a parliamentarian is clear.

Pages 24 & 25 is an article entitled "Atlantic Quest" by R. Burmaster who was a crew member on one of a number of Cruisers whose task was to attack the great German battleship 'Graf Spey'. An RAF Walrus amphibious bi-plane was to be launched by catapult from the cruiser. The pilot was his friend Dickie who the night before, during a game of cards, had been moaning about the lack of action. During the game Dickie got a message saying that he would be in flying the next morning. A Walrus had a crew of 3 and would be fired off by catapult whilst fully bomb laden. Burmaster tells the story.

——

Roll of Honour

C/JX 232568 Ord. Sig. E. A. Howard.   JX 179947 L. Sig. J. Bartholomew.

Honours and Awards

O.B.E.

Commander W. J. Rice,   R.D., R.N.R.   Captain F. W. Russell   (Sun V).
Commander L. Newman,   R.N.R.   Captain S. W. Smith (Sun VIII).

M.B.E.

Sig. Boatswain H.H.S. Wightman, R.N.   Chief Engineer A.P. Muirhead (Sun V).

D.S.C.

Lieut. C. Paget Clarke, R.N.V.R.

Mentioned in Despatches.

Comdr. D.T.M. Williams,   R.D., R.N.R.   Lieut. A. L. Adler, R.N.V.R.
Lieut. T. M. Rumbold,   R.N.V.R.   Chief Yeoman of Signals
         (Posthumous)   J. W. Lancaster.
Yeoman of Signals   A. Carter.   Signalman E. H. Sims.

Sub. Lieut. H. Downs has been presented with a Testimonial on Vellum by the Royal Humane Society for his plucky rescue of the Master of S.S. "Glendening", who whilst embarking, fell overboard between a tug and his ship. Lieut. Downs immediately jumped overboard and held him up until he was pulled aboard the tug. Both were in danger of being crushed between tug and ship.

(Continued on page 30).

- 2 -

Southend buys a destroyer

Not for the first time has Southend set the fashion, and now the whole country is about to follow Southend's lead with Navy Weeks. We called it a War Weapons Week like many others that have gone before, but having persuaded the First Lord to open the celebrations it was decided to raise enough money to buy a corvette. As everyone knows Southend is in a "protected" area and also, as everyone knows, Southend is very hard up, so that although a corvette as Naval Vessels go, is quite a small fellow it did represent quite a hefty target for Southend. Yes, Southend set out to raise £325,000 in a week – Southend did raise £524,833, so that after all, the duckling grew into a swan and Southend has bought a Destroyer. In this achievement we are glad and proud to say that the Navy paid no mean part and the enthusiasm shown on all sides by officers and ratings and not the least by our very smart Wren contingent took many practical forms.

War Weapons Week was opened officially by the First Lord when he took the salute at the Grand March Past of all the Fighting and Municipal Services in the town, on the brilliant Saturday afternoon of the 12th July but for the previous week there had been a great stir of preparation, not only behind the scenes but by the public itself. On the Monday, Captain Champion, with the Deputy Mayor in the Chair, opened the Naval Exhibition at Garons Center House, the proceeds of which contributed not a little towards the expenses of the week, so that all expenses were paid and a handsome cheque passed on to the Chancellor of the Exchequer in addition as a gift from the town, without touching the money raised towards our destroyer. It was on this occasion that Captain Champion, in his speech, set the goal for the town to purchase a corvette.

On the official opening day, the Rt. Hon. A. V. Alexander took his stand on the dais at the Cliffs Bandstand. The Royal Marine Band from Chatham led the procession followed by Training Class No.6 of the Thames Naval Control, who marched with fixed bayonets with Lieut. Moray in command. Following the Navy came a contingent of the Royal Maritime A.A. Artillery, whose good works in East Coast Convoys are so well known, then Army Units followed again by the R.A.F. contingents led by the kilted pipe band. After the R.A.F. came the Civilian Defence and Municipal Services each with their own particular characteristics and interspersed along the whole procession a variety of war weapons ancient and modern,

- 3 -

44

that is, 1914-18 and 1939-41.   The women's sections were again led by the Navy in the form of the W.R.N.S. contingent, whose blue skirts and white blouses made a really effective and conspicuous unit in the procession. It was pleasant to hear, both on this and on other occasions during the week when the Navy took part in the various processions, many jurisdictional remarks upon the bearing and smartness of the Thames Naval Control Training Class and the Southend W.R.N.S. contingent.

A Drumhead Service was held at Chalkwell Park on the following Sunday, conducted by Archdeacon Gowing of Southend, which was followed by a march past the Lord Lieutenant of the County, Colonel Sir Francis H.C.D. Whitmore, when the First Lieutenant was in command, and this party of some three thousand persons from all the services in the town was under the command of Captain Champion.

During the week, the Navy played its part in various ways and notable help was given by some of the Commodores of Convoys and the First Lieutenant, when they made appeals from the cinema platforms.   Here is an extract from one of these addresses and it is as well worth reading now as it was when Commander Bennett made his appeal:-

"Here in Southend we all see a lot of ships and everybody knows something about convoys. We hear a great deal about ships now-a-days; the Germans claim to be sinking thousands of tons; but no one hears much about the sailors. Convoys need protection so corvettes and convoys go together, and that's why we are hoping that Southend's War Weapons Week will raise enough to pay for a corvette.   All that a great number of people in England know about sailors is that they don't care and what the nice girls think about them.   Well - they don't care, but it isn't pleasant being bombed in convoy unless you have adequate protection and the means of hitting back. Cargoes are sailors' lives, so we've all been asked to use as little as possible of those commodities that come from overseas.   Very well then, if we're not spending the money on those things we can give a little of it to help the sailors and to make Southend's War Weapons Week and Help the Sailors Week................."

In his orders before Trafalgar, Admiral Nelson wrote: "If signals cannot be seen, no Captain can do wrong who lays his ship alongside one of the enemy"; and throughout the action he kept the signal flying, "Engage the enemy more closely".

We can always get the men. England goes to sea, and they don't come only from the seaport towns. They come from the countryside and the midlands, from Scotland, Wales and Ireland. But we must have the ships and guns. Please, next time you read anything about ships, think of the sailors. Think of the sugar, tea, the tobacco and the petrol (go easy on that petrol), that comes from overseas, and remember they are costing sailors' lives.

- 4 -

A fine model in wood of a corvette, Southend's aim for War Weapons Week, which was displayed outside the Municipal College, Victoria Circus, Southend.

Sailors formed a guard of honour for Capt. J. P. Champion, D.S.O., R.N., photographed with the Deputy Mayor (Ald. A. H. White) and Coun. J. E. Longman, J.P., when he opened the Naval Exhibition at Garon's Center House.

The Rt. Hon. A. V. Alexander, M.P., First Lord of the Admiralty, speaking at the opening of Southend's War Weapons Week.

All branches of the Services took part in the march-past on the Cliffs, when the salute was taken by the First Lord of the Admiralty.

At the march-past, after the Drumhead Service held at Chalkwell Park the salute was taken by Col. Sir Francis Whitmore, K.C.B., C.M.G., D.S.O., T.D., J.P., Lord Lieutenant of Essex.

The Home Guard marching past the saluting base on Saturday. Captain Champion, D.S.O., R.N., took the salute.

The Band of the Royal Marines in the Procession at the conclusion of War Weapons Week.

OLD WOODEN STOCK ANCHOR.

This Old Wooden Stock Anchor was recovered from the anchorage near West Shoebury Buoy by the steam drifter Lord Anson. Sir Geoffrey Callender, the Director of the National Maritime Museum, was asked to give an opinion as to its age, and he has replied, " The anchor has only one fluke and an antique shackle. From these clues I pronounce it old, when Nelson first went to sea, in the early Nineteenth Century. It was converted into a mooring anchor, and took down with it one of the early chain cables before these had been sanctioned by their lordships for ocean-going ships, i.e., 1817-19.". The final disposal of this anchor has not yet been decided, but, meanwhile, it fills a fitting position on the small plot in front of the Captain's Office (No. 8).

The Southend War Weapons Week Beauty Queen Contest was held nightly at the Regal Theatre, Tyler's Avenue, for a week, and ended with the selection, by popular vote, of Miss May Brien, aged 17, of Southend.

PHOTOGRAPHS loaned by the Proprietors of " The Southend Standard."

Now then, Southend, engage the enemy more closely. Instead of one corvette, why not make it two!"

When Saturday, 19th July arrived, the half million mark had been passed and Southend braced itself for a final effort. A grand march past again took place, the saluting base being St. Mary's Church, Prittlewell, where the salute was taken by Captain Champion. On this occasion, the Naval Training Class lead the procession with the W.R.N.S. contingent immediately following, the party being under the command of the First Lieut. Though we say it as shouldn't, it was the universal opinion of the spectators that the Naval contingent was outstanding in bearing and smartness. Incidentally, four of the ratings who took part have now passed through their Officers' course in "King Alfred" and have worthily maintained the Southend record of 100% passes.

For the town, the results of the week's work were far better than anticipated and the Navy's contribution has been suitably and generously acknowledged by the General Executive Committee under the Mayor of Southend, Alderman W. Miles, O.B.E., J.P., in a letter of thanks in which a sum of £50 was contributed towards the Thames Naval Control Fund in the following words :-

"From this surplus it was decided to contribute the sum of £100 to the Benevolent Funds of each of the three Services, in grateful recognition of the assistance rendered by Officers and personnel throughout the week. Accordingly, it is with considerable pleasure as President of the Week and on behalf of the General Executive Committee, that I enclose two cheques for £50, - one for the Thames Naval Control Fund, and the other for the Royal Naval War Amenities Fund, which I think you may like to send direct to the Secretary."

This generous gift comes at a time when the demands on the Thames Naval Control Welfare Fund are beginning to mount up with the approach of winter. In expressing our appreciation of this practical recognition of the Navy's help we can sincerely say "WELL DONE SOUTHEND!"

-----ooo0ooo-----

A revolutionary system of sailing convoys has been formulated by the Pier Tram Driver in co-operation with his skilled assistant. This is said to involve a policy of sailing stern first to mislead enemy aircraft.

- 5 -

The old House of Commons, familiar to all Londoners and provincials for the past one hundred years, was obliterated by German bombs in May of this year, but Parliament's temporary home is also accessible from Southend. One September morning, when the familiar note of XG was sounding round the Anchorage, I realised that it also had a personal application and caught the early train to town.

Fenchurch Street has always seemed to me the threshold of our Base and on this occasion it lived up to its reputation. At the Barrier I found four of our Signalmen on their way to the mysteries and exertions of the Officers' Course at "King Alfred", while in the other direction could be seen a Commodore and his staff, pie-eyed after an all night train journey from the north. To those arriving at this early hour, I can recommend the ministrations of Toc H, which lies a stone's throw from P.L.A. Building, and provides an excellent breakfast in the shortest possible time.

After looking in on N.C.S.O. London, I made my way to the Western Hemisphere and soon encountered familiar faces in the political world, making their way to the first sitting of the House following the short August recess. It is always comforting and gives a sense of the eternal continuity of our affairs to find, even in the midst of our most critical war, the age long ritual being carried out; the stately Speaker's procession; the Chaplain reading the prayers which have been in daily use since the Restoration in 1660, and the sound tradition under which no Government business can be taken until Private Members have had their chance to interrogate Ministers.

On this day, question time was largely occupied with such matters as the Armistice terms in Syria and Iran, but Parliament has always reflected national interest in matters much nearer home. On this occasion the Government had to undergo a sharp bout of heckling regarding Service pay and allowances, and it was immediately clear that strong feeling existed on both sides of the House. Indeed, the Treasury Bench was soon exposed to a breeze by no means gentle, which seemed to surprise Ministers but made them conscious of an issue which must soon be faced. It is an excellent example of the manner in which the Executive is kept in touch with the Man-in-the-Street under a democratic system such as ours. Question time, however, was nothing more than a curtain raiser to the chief event of the day, the Prime Minister's statement on the progress of the War. This was Mr. Churchill's first appearance since his Atlantic Voyage to meet President Roosevelt, and it was fitting therefore, that his speech

- 21 -

should begin with a survey of the sea war. He had an encouraging story to tell of a sharp decline in British and Allied shipping losses combined with an almost dramatic increase in the sinkings of enemy tonnage. It was very pleasing to hear the Prime Minister go out of his way to pay tribute to the Officers and Men of the Minesweeping Service, whose dull daily routine passes unnoticed for weeks and months at a time. The story of counter action against magnetic and acoustic mines is familiar to readers of "SPUN YARN", but the public of course is not so well informed. Mr. Churchill ended this part of his review by quoting Kipling's impressive lines written during the last war:-

> "Mines reported in the fairway
> "Warn all traffic and detain
> "Send up UNITY, CLARIBEL, ASSYRIAN
> "STORMCOCK and GOLDEN GAIN."

From here Mr. Churchill switched to the vast and critical battle of Russia, then at its height, pointing out that the German casualties in two months had exceeded those in any single year of 1914 to 1918, and promising all material assistance from this country although we should have to go short of supplies ourselves in consequence.

Perhaps, however, the most intriguing feature of the speech was something which it did not contain. The long heralded invasion of our island, for which we have been warned to prepare so often, did not receive mention even in a single sentence.

When the Prime Minister sat down, there was the usual exodus to the Lobby to discuss his statement and compare notes, but Parliament does not function in the debating chamber alone. For instance, I attended a committee of private members which is perhaps, a typical example of the British democratic system - it certainly could not happen in Germany! This body was convened by Petty Officer A. P. Herbert who presided over Admiral of the Fleet Sir Roger Keyes, Admiral Sir Percy Royds, Rear Admiral Beamish, Lord Winterton, Viscountess Astor and a few more of us. Our aim, which I am sure commends itself to all who have had any contact with the Naval Control Service, is to suggest measures for raising the status and improving the general position of the Mercantile Marine, particularly with a view to regulating the employment of its officers and men in war and peace. "And so," as Pepys would say - Back to Southend, well in time to sign the Night Order Book and return to the familiar routine.

-----oooOooo-----

Notice seen pinned on Pay Office door:

> "NEVER HAVE SO MANY WAITED
> FOR SO LONG FOR SO LITTLE."

- 22 -

Atlantic Quest

by R. Burmester

H.M.S. "X" was under sailing orders.   In an hour or two the hands were to fall in for leaving harbour; strolling down the little dockyard road, in the afternoon sunshine, I met "Dickie", placidly walking towards the dockyard gates.   He pulled up, and in his pleasant drawl invited me to come and inspect his newly conditioned aircraft.

"I don't get enough flying, blast it", he voiced the old and honest complaint of the cruiser airman, who often flies only as many hours in a month as an R.A.F. pilot flies per diem.

"Maybe you'll go up tomorrow", I answered.

With a disconsolate grunt Dickie went on his way.

The same evening, when the last remnants of Ward Room supper had been cleared from the long rectangular table, the "bridge" four settled down in opposition to a nearby table of Mah Jongh, "Bish" and I opened a successful partnership against Dickie and the P.M.O.   We were suddenly interrupted by the handing of a message to Dickie, who outwardly betrayed little of the enthusiasm he must have felt - on the morrow he was to fly.

. . . .

It was a fine morning of bright sunshine, and the blue sky curved at the horizon to join the white-capped Atlantic rollers.   The prepara- tions for catapulting the "Walrus" aircraft had attracted the customary audience.

I walked for'ard from the quarter deck, and climbed the ladder to the 4 inch gun deck.   Here, just aft of a long cigarette-shaped funnel, perched formidably upon a narrow steel structure was the squat,   canoe- like aircraft.   Its spread wings were now loaded with bombs in racks on the under side.   A little group of officers and men directly responsible for the despatch of the aircraft watched the crew climb awkwardly into the cockpit.   The aircraft slid slowly back like an arrow drawn tight against a bow string, to the limit of the steel runway.   A hand-flag dropped; Dickie's gloved arm signalled ready, and there was a hiss like

- 24 -

the starting of a firework.   And now the engine throttled to crescendo. Away sped the machine, its path an upward trajectory.   Dickie, after the moment's inevitable loss of consciousness which follows catapulting, took control of the machine and climbed away until the ship was a toy beneath him.

That same evening, after dinner, Dickie's place at the bridge table was taken by another officer.   There was a buzz that the aircraft was overdue, for its endurance was only a few hours flying.   It was rumoured in the Ward Room that an indistinct and indecypherable report of the 'plane's whereabouts feebly tapped out by the nervous fingers of the lieutenant-observer indicated that they were off their course and off their bearings. The under-charged batteries were failing in their function.   All too soon the W/T operator reported that the dying S.O.S. was dead, and as we altered course with our grey sister cruiser, the news spread that our captain was abandoning the search for the German battleship "Graf Spee" and beginning a search for the missing trio and their aircraft.

For the next few days, the sailors, the marine servants who min-istered the early morning cups of tea and shaving-water, the bronzed young snotties, the doctors, and the chaplain passed hours of anxious wondering. Everyone volunteered to take his turn as look-out...... climbing into the high, mushroom-shaped A.D.P. look-out post and gazing into the infinity of sea and sky, with the monster service binoculars. A watch that was in vain.   Even this grim business yielded its moment of humour. The captain of our sister ship came one day to consult his "oppo", missed his footing between the hastily-lowered ladder and the ferrying motor-boat and stepped into the "drink".   Rescued, the little man, a creased and bedraggled fig-ure, was greeted by our skipper with ......"Ah!   Not house-trained yet I see!"

The vain and bitter days of search for the missing "Walrus" closed on a Sunday.   A day of grey skies and heavy rollers which viciously rocked our ship from side to side, so that the paraded ranks of sailors awaiting divisions, found no easy foothold.   After a short and appropriate com-memoration service, the Captain told the assembled ship's company of the thorough search that had been made by the companion cruisers, our sister ship and her aircraft.   But the sea had kept its cruel secret well and had given up no trace of Dickie, his crew or the aircraft.

The Captain hazarded at their probable fate...... a forced landing in the turbulent wind-whipped sea which would have caused the bomb-laden rack to blow up, thereby instantly destroying its crew - a death whose only merit was its quickness as opposed to the slow starvation which would otherwise have been their fate.

We were all rather quiet that day, as each man in his own way thought of the first loss of the war.

- 25 -

SPUN-YARN

1942 ★ FEBRUARY. ★ 1942

The Journal of the Thames Naval Control.

N. Sotheby Pitcher.
1942

Lorient in North West France is a port on the upper river Loire leading out to the Atlantic. After Dunkirk and the fall of Paris there was panic and fugitives in their thousands fled ahead of the Germans advancing through Northern France. They headed for Lorient to seek escape in one of the British Ships anchored there. NCS officers Commander R. V. Rutley and Lieut. Shaw of NCS Southend were selected by The Admiralty to assist the escape of our shipping (laden with fugitives) in the port of Lorient before arrival of the German army.

Pages 3 - 5 of this edition of Spun Yarn tells the story of "Retreat from Lorient" and the heroic and successful achievement of Rutley and Shaw. The Germans arrived in Lorient only hours after the successful departure of our ships in spite of German aircraft laying mines in their path to prevent them.

In German hands Lorient was to become the established base for U-boats in the battle of The Atlantic. The RAF bombed the site almost out of existence except that the Germans had constructed a bomb proof harbour for their U-boats which was never breached.

Southend Base Ships Club - pages 6 and 7

Captain Champion was a great motivator and a very good organiser. He realised the importance of offering off-duty relief to the many army and navy personnel. His wisdom and ingenuity was used to create a facility through which socialising brought people together. This would in turn make for easier friendly cooperation in the wartime business of convoy work.

Football, cricket and tennis matches were arranged against local clubs and inter-forces teams. The rear rooms behind St. John's Church at the back of the Palace Hotel were made into a club with darts, snooker and most importantly, shows. There were pantomimes put on where servicemen often dressed up as women. Captain Jenkins made a wonderful Carmen Miranda with a WREN's undergarment around his head as a turban on top of which were vegetables instead of fruit. On base Capt. Jenkins was something of a character. He stayed after the war and became Commodore of the Alexander Yacht Club. His daughter today lives in Westcliff.

The Club that Capt. Champion created was called SBSC (Southend Base Ships Club). They even had their own club base song. The first line was "The Southend Base, the Convoy Base, Lord Haw Haw says he knows the place"

Pages 8 & 9 entitled "The Sponsors" was especially contributed to Spun Yarn by Admiral R. A. Hopwood CB., author of 'The Laws of the Navy'.

Page 10 is selected for the second item on the page, a humorous take on the "Observation Post" whose job was to keep watch for enemy aircraft.

Copied from page 19

- Medical Officer to new conscript. "Sick? Rot! Would you have come to me like this in peace-time?" New Conscript. "No sir, I would have sent for you".

Page 22 is included for the cartoon of Lord Haw Haw.

—————

RETREAT FROM LORIENT
BY N.B.

The events as related to N.B.

The break through at Sedan, Dunkirk evacuation and the fall of Paris laid North Western France open to the invader. The dreary tale of retreat now revealed itself in panic flight. Broken armies and broken-hearted refugees poured south and west varied only by valiant bands selling their lives dearly that others might escape. Even so, breakdown of transport and exhaustion resulted in thinning out the fleeing columns, thus as the Atlantic approached, roads became less blocked and normal conditions returned. But one fugitive out-stripped all others, spreading despair in every village through which he passed; his name was Rumour, and in his mouth companies were swollen to divisions, cyclists were tanks, ignorance brought confusion and confusion panic.

It was in such circumstances that Commander Rutley and Lieut. Shaw arrived in Nantes one sunny day in June. They had been selected from the Thames Naval Control by the Admiralty. The party left Hendon at 0200 and made a clean start for Nantes on the River Loire. The Aerodrome at which they landed five hours after leaving Hendon was in the hands of a Canadian fighter squadron who invited the party to a welcome breakfast. But transport to Lorient, the party's final destination, was not to be had. The town itself was packed with fugitives, the Consulate being besieged by hundreds wanting passage to England. Commander Rutley after some delay was able to see the British Consul and was put in touch with a Mr. & Mrs. Browning and their family of two sons and a daughter, whose help was to prove invaluable in the work that lay ahead. The boys made themselves useful as messengers and, being able to speak French fluently, also as interpreters between the party and excited Frenchmen of all kinds, but best of all their **father** owned two cars. So they set out through thinning crowds of refugees and abandoned cars, passing British troops and transport, tired and worn with ceaseless fighting and marching on their way to the coast. At 1700 they arrived at Lorient where Commander Rutley set up the first British Naval Control Service Office in the Port. The Brownings proved of immense help now; the clerical work fell to the daughter, a competent typist, while the boys were sent on errands. Next day young John brought in six swarthy Breton fishermen to whom he had been talking on the Quay. They willingly agreed to see "Le Commandant" and very loyal and valuable they proved to

- 3 -

be.   Later the British Consul,   Mr. King, arrived so that with   Doctor Browning and her husband, Commander Rutley now had three responsible people on whom he could rely.

Leaving the Doctor to hold the fort,   the First Lieutenant,   Mr. Browning and Mr. King with two Breton fishermen, the brothers Paul and Adrien went in one of the cars   to board British and Neutral vessels alongside Meantime Rutley tried to phone the British Captains at Brest and Nantes;   but all the lines were out.   Later the Consul and Commander Rutley went to see the French Port Admiral, but all sorts of impediments were raised.   Just as they were beginning to think the obstruction deliberate they met Lieut-de-Vaisseau Carlier.   This Officer once lived in England and was very friendly. An interview with the Admiral was fixed for next morning and they   returned to their Hotel stopping to obtain permits from the Security Police on their way.   At 0200 on Thursday, 24 hours after leaving the Admiralty they turned in weary, but with the satisfaction of a day's work well and truly done.

As he lay on the edge of sleep turning over in his mind the kaleido-scopic succession of the day's scenes, Rutley became conscious of   the magnitude of the tragedy which had befallen our Ally.   For the first   time he realised that except for these half dozen Breton fishermen he had   not seen a young Frenchman out of uniform.   He remembered too, though at the time he had not particularly noticed, a group of women at work in the fields outside Redon;   then there was that girl in charge of the Level   Crossing and the young woman driving heavy lorries they passed the day before.   All these and other incidents brought home to him the outstanding fact that France had put her all into the fight, had stretched her man power to the   utmost and that having done all and failed was now looking defeat in the face.

Bright and early next morning, King and Rutley drove   through   the Dockyard Gates.   The Admiral was a short stoutish man from a Southern Province in his late 50s.   The interview was short but Commander Rutley obtained an assurance of co-operation and returned to his Headquarters.   His staff had by now boarded every ship in harbour, and British and Neutral captains were to report at 1000 next day.   However,   it was now found possible to clear six ships, including two tankers, and these left heavily laden   for British Ports.

The second day approached its close to the sound of siren and within 10 minutes Lorient was experiencing its first "blitz".   King and Rutley went to the Consulate where a cypher message from the Admiralty was waiting. Unfortunately it was so mutilated as to be undecipherable.   To add to the difficulty all lights were cut off at the main.   So they decided to return to the Hotel and all but ended this story by driving into a pile of masonry in mistake for shadows.   They continued to struggle with the message but gave up when a bomb on the station opposite shattered all the windows   and made further work impossible. The devastation in the Town next morning was appalling but little damage was done to shipping in the harbour.   After a hurried breakfast Commander Rutley prepared to receive the British Masters, but was interrupted by Paul and Adrien, who reported that during the blitz

- 4 -

they had been out in a boat and observed numbers of mines dropped. This was serious, for many ships had to be got away at all costs, most of them packed with refugees. There was no time to be lost; the planes would return and as it was there was a likelihood of losing a number of these vessels in attempting to escape. Moreover, French Warships were in Harbour and Rutley's instructions were to try and persuade the French Admiral to send them to Plymouth. Rutley used all his powers to persuade the obstinate Frenchman. The most he would say at first was "the Boche shall not get them", but Rutley pressed for something more definite and at last was told they would go to North Africa. The Germans were now reported only 60 kilometers away. This meant they had less than two hours! Rutley suggested the immediate blowing up of the River Bridge and demolition of petrol tanks. French obstinancy here proved unsurmountable: the spirit that sacrificed Paris forbade the Admiral to injure "La Belle Lorient"! Rutley could only hope his warning would register in time!

Rutley now arranged to leave. Lieut. Carlier had placed a fast picket boat at his disposal and Rutley boarded his ship, made the signal to "Weigh", and soon they were snaking around the red dan buoys marking enemy mines. The merchantmen were followed by Cruisers and Destroyers which steamed South - the Admiral had kept his word! As the large ships steamed out they passed many vessels loaded down with refugees; small craft were towed by tugs; yachts and barges, all carrying full live cargoes and as he saw them Rutley prayed for fine weather.

Before embarking the party said farewell to the stalwart Breton fishermen to whom so much of their success was due, who represented the unconquerable spirit of French resistance. To Paul and Adrien Commander Rutley committed a final mission. The bridge was intact, the oil tanks full and undamaged. They must be destroyed! The offer of the party's cash was refused indignantly by the Bretons, who stated that only for the honour of France would they do the work. As the leading ship passed between the forts a shattering detonation rent the air and a few minutes afterwards the petrol tanks burst into flame - the honour of France had inspired the deed! And so the motley convoy sailed out into the Bay of Biscay. They were blessed with fine weather, but towards dusk a plane was spotted and without protection there was only one thing to do: the Masters knew their orders and after dark scattered and proceeded independently. Every ship arrived at it's allotted English Port - the evacuation of Lorient was complete.

The names given other than British Naval Officers are fictitious.

EDITORS NOTE:-   We should like to express our appreciation
to H.H. Burrows, Esq., of the " Southend
Standard " for the Press Photographs of the
War Weapons Week, published in our last issue.

- 5 -

In taking this opportunity of wishing all our friends a very happy New Year, we can also review the progress made by our Ship's Club during the three months since its opening on October 1st, by the Captain.

We feel that in these three months we have achieved at least one of the aims with which we began; getting everyone in the Base to meet outside duty hours, enjoying evenings together, and so getting to know one another very much better. In doing this we have discovered much previously hidden talent, as the following short description of the opening concert, written by Payr. Lieut. W. S. Joseph, will show

"In honour of the inauguration of the Ship's Club by the Captain, the Committee put on a Singsong which, judging by its reception, was a veritable success. As is customary on first nights, the curtain rose six minutes late on a stage well lit and nicely decorated. The promoters suffered from no dearth of talent and presented a programme full of originality and good acts.

The naval performers were all excellent and it is an invidious task to draw distinctions; as Dogberry says, "Comparisons are odourous." However, on my own head............... The audience enjoyed the banjulele experts, O.Sig. (George Formby) Freeborn and Writer Griffiths, with whom we lustily joined in the choruses. Everyone, from the Captain to the ship's boy, rocked with mirth over the extremely clever "Good enough for Punch" recitation of Sig. Faulks. Writer Beckwith (surely a member of the Magic Circle?) with a dummy from the audience, mystified us completely with clever card tricks. Wren Saunders sang prettily and looked (if it may be said) even more charming in her lavender evening gown. Surg. Lt. MacBane, without any apologies given or needed to Stanley Holloway, enrolled young Albert in the ranks of Convoy Signalmen, to our considerable amusement, not least that of the 1st Lieutenant.

- 6 -

The piece de resistance of the evening, if among so much talent anyone could be said to stand out from among the others, was Lieut. Hemery, ably accompanied by L. Sig. Yates.   Though his act seemed to lack enough rehearsal, this gentleman has a magnificent voice although at times, he, like an even more distinguished artist whom he very cleverly imitated, uses it for purposes not always written in the score.

All in all, it was a magnificent show and special words of praise are due to Lieut. Moray, our able compere for his amusing introductions and to the producer and stage manager, O. Sig. Norman C. Harrill, who despite what may have gone on back stage, produced an extremely slick show to us in front."

The Club was well patronized after this, and on October 16th twelve of our members visited the Southend Police Recreational Club and played them at snooker and darts.   Refreshments were provided and everyone thoroughly enjoyed himself.

On November 20th, a dozen Chief P.O's, P.O's and Leading Rates visited the Maritime Artillery Sergeant's Mess and greatly enjoyed a very entertaining evening.

On the evening of November 26th, a concert given at the Club by the Co-odments Concert Party was well attended by officers, ratings and their friends.   The Captain, who was present, proposed a vote of thanks at the end of a very good show.

On December 10th, Mr. Tate, a resident of Southend, very kindly gave us a Cinematograph Show, and though the attendance for this was small, yet those present enjoyed a very good two hours entertainment.   The film of the Capture of Zeebrugge Mole in the last war was especially appreciated.

December 17th saw the opening of the Club Canteen, staffed by the W.V.S., and as this coincided with the recovering of the billiard table we were able to return the hospitality of the Police Force.

With the club now well established, and the canteen and billiard table both in full swing, we propose to go ahead with many matches at darts, billiards, etc. with our friends outside, and competitions amongst ourselves.

We welcome all suggestions for improving the club in any way, so just write a note and leave it with the duty committee man of an evening, and meanwhile we hope you will continue to come along and enjoy yourselves.

Now that a certain officer has reaped the fruits and vegetables of his labours at the rear of the Base, the alterations have been allowed to proceed without further delay.

- 7 -

The Sponsors

ESPECIALLY CONTRIBUTED TO SPUN YARN — BY ADMIRAL R A HOPWOOD CB AUTHOR OF THE LAWS OF THE NAVY —

O Thou that sittest above the water floods and stillest the raging of the sea, accept, we beseech Thee, the supplications of Thy servants for all who, in this ship, now and hereafter, shall commit their lives unto the perils of the deep. In all their ways enable them truly and godly to serve Thee, and by their Christian lives to set forth Thy glory throughout the earth.

> Prayer used at the Launching of
> Ships of His Majesty's Navy.

Lest any forget how the waters were moved
    Ere Light over Chaos the victory won,
'Tis meet that a ship, of her sponsors approved,
    Be hallowed ere free to give service thereon.
A service whose span is the length of her days -
    A freedom - whose price is the service she pays.

So there, on her cradle, behold her arrayed,
    And when was a babe to such destiny born?
The flag of the Empire above her displayed,
    And when was a robe of such ancestry worn?
Its emblems were old ere the Empire was new:
    Three Crosses aflame in a firmament blue.

Her name has been sealed by the wine on her stem,
    A great cloud of witnesses hangs on her mood,
She pauses, but scant is her homage to them,
    For deep calls to deep - with the last of the flood -
A challenge, prophetic of peril - and peace:
    "Who sponsors this ship that we grant her release?"

A fisherman speaks: "To whatever appeal
    "She hastens, obeying the Laws of the Sea
"Her works shall discover her faith and reveal
    "The reason a Ship seemeth hallowed to me
"I bid you release her to Witness and Praise,
    "St. Andrew is sponsor in all of her ways."

- 8 -

Then knightly comes answer: "My conquering sign
    "Shall fly at her topmast and, steeling her nerve
"Confound a more sinister dragon than mine,
    "I pledge her new power - the power to Serve.
"St. George is her sponsor by day and by night,
    "Who bids you release her to fight a good fight."

A herdsman replies: "To the Isle of Distress
    "The Cross was my summons, to shepherd and guide,
"Though brimming and bitter our tears, none the less
    "Praise be, we'd a sweet'ning of laughter beside!
"'Tis I bid you loose her to Sorrow - and Mirth,
    "St. Patrick, her sponsor all over the earth."

Unconsciously spellbound the witnesses wait
    Till, waked to her birthright, she quivers and moves
Then gliding with graceful and quickening gait,
    As one seeking peace on a breast that she loves,
'Mid cheering and music she's clasped by the seas,
    Now when did a babe have such sponsors as these?

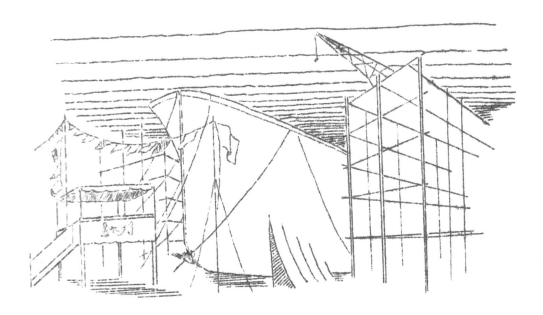

- 9 -

General Knowledge

AMV + TK + GA = FLAP

OR DO·U·NO

"The glass is rising" means someone is tipping their elbow.

"The four seasons" - Salt, Mustard, Vinegar, Pepper.

"Days are longer in summer than winter because heat expands everything."

"The Temperate Zone is the region where no one drinks too much."

"Marconi is used for making puddings."

"A Magnet is a thing you find in bad apples."

⚓ ⚓ ⚓ ⚓ ⚓

OBSERVATION POST ~
· · SCENE I · ·

Officer, scanning the horizon through his glasses, suddenly starts and says, "Private Smith, take this message."

"Enemy forces in large numbers approaching the coast, range 10,000 yards, light and heavy Naval units and approximately 5 to 10 thousand barges in tow, supported by troop carriers, dive bombers, fighters in huge numbers, visibility good, wind South West, gentle breeze, sea slight."

"Got that, Private Smith?"

"Yes, sir."

"Are you certain, Smith?"

"Yes, sir."

"Very good, transmit."

SCENE II.

Private Smith on the 'phone.   "Is that you, Alf?"

"Yes Bert, what is it?"

"You can ring the ruddy bells, the b........ are here!"

- 10 -

Their comments may be summarised as follows:-

"All very nice for the industrial workers but where is the Service man's nest egg coming from? Why should his wife have one long grim fight to maintain her home while wives of munition workers are better off than before the war? Why the discrimination against His Majesty's Forces? The Chancellor is ignoring the Services because they are not and cannot be vocal.   The Government must think again."

The attack grew in strength and ended in a pledge from Mr. Attlee the Lord Privy Seal, that the whole question of the discrepancy in pay between the Forces and Industry together with the problem of nest eggs for men who come out of the Services at the end of the war would be carefully examined by a Committee and a report made to the House as soon as possible in the New Year. Thus did the Government seasonably follow the routine laid down by Good King Wenceslas who, it will be recalled, postponed his benevolent activities until the Feast of Stephen, although he must have realised that many of his less fortunate subjects were in need on Christmas Day.   "Still, better late than never," thought the House, and with this assurance His Majesty got his Thousand Millions.

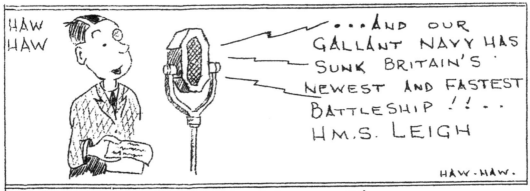

(continued from page 12).

We must mention here the really fine work put in throughout, by the Maritime A.A. Orchestra, who not only played according to their score, but gallantly stepped into every breach and breakdown, and so ensured a smooth running performance.

We should also like to pay tribute to the very fine work of the Stage Manager (Sig. Hammill), L.Sig. Nottage, and all those who worked really hard behind the scenes to make this the successful evening that it undoubtedly was.

EDITORS NOTE: We are very much obliged to the First Lieut. for so kindly giving "Spun Yarn" free advertisement in his prologue.

- 22 -

- SPUN-YARN -

The Journal of the Thames Naval Control.

★ ★

Special Feature :

1000TH CONVOY SAILS FROM
THE THAMES ESTUARY

PRICE SIXPENCE. ★ SEPTEMBER ★ 1942.

Honours and Awards on page 2 highlights an OBE for Commander R. V. Rutley; There is a KBE for Vice Admiral F. M. Austin and a Mentioned in Despatches for NCS Lieut. I. M. Burt and Yeoman of Signals L. F. Matthews.

Pages 3 & 4 headed "1000 CONVOYS" contains congratulations from their Lordships at The Admiralty and a review of NCS operations to date.

Page 9 is an article detailing the history and origins of the Naval Salute (shading of the eyes)

Pages 12 - 14 give an account of the "1000th Convoy Dinner at Garons Restaurant with 35 officers present. Tributes were paid to the first NCSO Capt. Roger Alison. After dinner speeches were made by various senior officers. There were congratulations for Capt. Champion.

Pages 18 - 21 is the account of Yeoman L. F. Matthews on the day to day routine of Southend convoy work for a Yeoman. Entitled "Escape", it is 4 pages of wonderful first-hand information and experience.

I have included page 28 - "Sports News" which is a continuation page but mentions the use of Thorpe Bay Tennis Club. This facility was made available to NCS members by Miss Royle of the Club's committee, whose address and telephone number are given. Capt. Champion was a keen tennis player and I wonder if he played locally during the war.

When researching John Champion I visited the village of Hasketon, Nr. Woodbridge in Suffolk on the River Deben. The house where he lived in 1939 before returning to naval duties is called Short Hoo. The very kind current owner Suzie Dolbey was aware that our Champion loved to play tennis and there was a court in the grounds of the house.

The Sutton Hoo burial ship discovered in 1939 was just a few miles away. Treasures found are now in the British Museum and are the greatest perfect examples of their kind from 2,000 years ago. John Champion would have been aware of this historic event on his doorstep.

Pages 29 - 32 is the story of 'a newcomer' working on the secret codes. Her article is entitled "Morning in the Cypher Office". It is another humorous but very informative account of one of the key activities on which there was permanent engagement at NCS Southend.

Pay. Lieut. G. B. Kidd, R.N.V.R.   Leading Sig. Jack Jennings.
Signalman W. B. Trevorrow.   Signalman C. W. J. Healey.

Honours and Awards

O.B.E.

Comdr. R.V. Rutley, R.D., R.N.R. (Retd.).   Comdr. C.W.C. Pinckney, R.D.,R.N.R.

B.E.M.

C.S.B. P.O. J. G. Cumber.

D.S.M.

Signalman R. F. C. Durbin.

Mentioned in Despatches.

Commander A. H. Dyer, R.N.R.   Lieut. I. M. Burt, R.N.V.R.
Yeoman of Signals J.R. Pegler
Yeoman of Signals L.F. Matthews
Yeoman of Signals O.R. Boucher

M.B.E. (Merchant Navy)

Captain J. H. Potts.   s.s. "BETSWOOD"

FORMERLY WITH THAMES NAVAL CONTROL.

K.B.E.

Vice Admiral F. M. Austin, C.B. (Retd.).

C.B.E.

Captain (Acting Commodore 2nd class) J. K. Brook, D.S.O., R.D.,R.N.R.

D.S.M.

Yeoman of Signals T. Clarke

Mentioned in Despatches.

T/Lieut. S.M. Booker, R.N.V.R. H.M.S. "GAVOTTE"

CONGRATULATIONS continued on page 7.

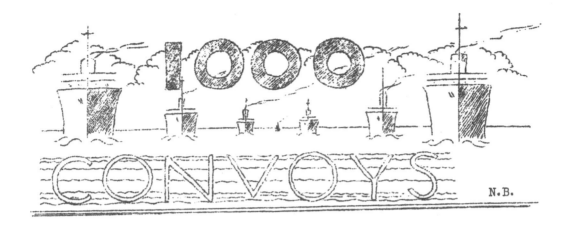

N.B.

"THEIR LORDSHIPS CONGRATULATE ALL CONCERNED ON THE SUCCESSFUL SAILING FROM THE THAMES OF 1000 EAST COAST, CHANNEL AND OCEAN CONVOYS WITH A LOSS OF LESS THAN HALF OF ONE PER CENT OF THE SHIPS CONVOYED."

An important land-mark for the Thames Naval Control was passed, when a convoy sailed for Orfordness and the North on the 7th May, 1942, and Captain Champion was able to report to the Commander-in-Chief, that the 1000th Convoy had been organised and had successfully passed the Nore. This achievement evoked the above quoted message of congratulations from the Admiralty, received by the Thames Naval Control with no small pride and satisfaction at having so effectively contributed to one of Britain's most vital war services.

It is also with much satisfaction that we recall a similar message received from Their Lordships within ten days of the outbreak of war when the Thames Naval Control succeeded in getting away on a single day and within a week of its outbreak, the first two convoys of the war.

Here is the message:-

"The expeditious organisation of convoys is a matter of much satisfaction to Their Lordships and reflects great credit on all concerned."

Thus the Thames Naval Control keeps up its reputation for good work as the months pass by, always with a lively feeling or urgency and a sense of responsibility for seeing that whatever is done is well done. That first convoy which sailed on the 7th September, 1939, bearing Admiral Lane Poole as Commodore, was not a large one, consisting of but eleven ships, mostly Colliers. But humble though they be, these small and slow, grimy and rusty Colliers pass to and fro along the East Coast of England, in the

- 3 -

very forefront of the battle defiantly braving the utmost that a savage enemy can do, with mines, bombs or cannon. Though here and there he may achieve success by the sinking of a ship or the destruction of a cargo, yet the staunch valour of her crew has brought many a sinking ship to safety, and thwarted the Hun in his most desperate efforts to cut Britain's Life Line.

It was a tragic day which saw the over-running of the French Channel Ports by the uncivilised Hun. Never before in history had England stood in such imminent danger. Even as the heroes of Dunkirk were being rescued from those perilous beaches, by the Navy, by the Merchantmen, and by the Fishermen and Yachtsmen from England's rivers and harbours from the Thames to the Wight, the last of the Ocean convoys was making its way up channel. It may indeed have seemed to some that henceforth the immemorial Straits of Dover were never again to witness the passage of the Red Ensign. But to hold such a view was to reckon without British resourcefulness or British courage! Within a matter of days a new Channel convoy, destined to maintain supplies to the southern English ports, was forging its way in the teeth of the enemy and into the very jaws of death, to keep the life line open. This Convoy sailed from the Thames on the 6th July, 1940.

Though many have sailed and returned since that date, as in East Coast Convoys, there are sad vacancies among the dauntless officers and men of these brave ships. Nevertheless their work goes on; the Unspeakable Hun is constantly frustrated, and must now know that his efforts are doomed to defeat.

We of the Thames Naval Control know, as no one else, how much Britain owes to the officers and men of our matchless Merchant Service and to our loyal Allies. With them we have formed a link of mutual confidence and understanding, and it can be said with pride there is not in our long records a single case of a Merchant Navy crew having failed to put to sea in the face of the enemy. The Merchant Navy officers and men would be the first to acknowledge the debt that they and England owe to the incomparable Escorts provided for their convoys by the Royal Navy, whose officers and men spend weary and exacting hours in shepherding their charges up the East Coast through 'E-Boat Alley' or through the perilous Straits of Dover.

Between the Merchant Navy and the Escorts, the Commodores supported by their staffs, occupy a position of unique responsibility. Among other things they interpret the instructions and directions which have been formulated or passed on by the Thames Naval Control, so that they personify the Navy in a particularly intimate fashion to the Merchant ships under their charge.

Thus has this trinity of co-operation by Escorts, Commodores and Naval Control Service been of one mind and purpose in ensuring the successful sailing and safe arrival of One Thousand Convoys from the Thames.

- 4 -

To-day, when all British people are playing a part in what will prove to be the most historic days in the History of Civilization, it is fitting to dwell from time to time on the formation of other historic events of the past.

There is no better time than during these difficult days, to think on the achievements and traditions of the fighting men of the past, whose spirit and fortitude lives in the men of to-day: Beneath everything else, every Britisher knows that this spirit lives within him and can never die.

We may remember the simplicity of the words of a great sailor, Sir Francis Drake when he wrote of his discovery of Cape Horn and his voyage round the world:-

"We safely, with joyful minds and thankful hearts to God, arrived at Plymouth, the place of our first setting forth, after we had spent two years, ten months and some odd days in seeing the wonders of the Lord in the deep, in discovering so many admirable things, in going through so many strange adventures, in escaping so many dangers, and overcoming so many difficulties in this, our encompassing of the globe and passing round the world."

Drake's famous order before setting out on that wonderful voyage ran something like this...... "The gentlemen will haul with the mariners, and the mariners with the gentlemen."

The little "Golden Hind" had returned, laden with silver and Drake was knighted on her quarter deck by Queen Elizabeth.   There is a legend attached to this visit to the "Golden Hind".

We are all acquainted with the great lady's facial characteristics and according to 1942 glamour girl's standards, know she was not too hand-some, but legend has it that prior to the Queen's arrival Drake issued an order to the effect that as soon as she stepped over the gangway, every man was to shade his eyes with his right hand lest "the sight of the Queen's dazzling beauty should blind him."

Drake was the first commissioned sea officer in any navy - and it has been said that from his order given on board the "Golden Hind" sprang the present day naval salute.

- 9 -

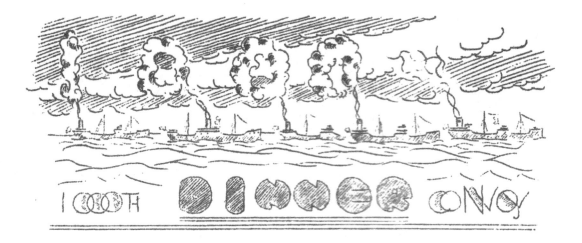

The sailing of our 1000th Convoy was celebrated by a dinner at Garon's Restaurant on Friday, 22nd May, to Captain Champion, being attended by 35 officers, many of whom have served in the Thames Naval Control since its early days.

This proved a most enjoyable function, and in addition to an exceptional menu, emphasised the spirit of comradeship and co-operation which has always characterised the T.N.C. The theme throughout was reminiscent - after-dinner speeches varied and studded with humour. After the loyal toast, Commander Marshall, who was in the chair, proposed the principal toast to Captain Champion. He dwelt on the chief incidents of the Captain's periods of Command and paid fitting tribute to his qualities and leadership, while pointing out that the disappointment of the Base on his departure (in September, 1940) was only equalled by the joy at his selection as Captain Goff's successor (in April, 1941). Commander Marshall went on to discuss the early story of the Thames Naval Control, and in the course of his remarks, said that Payr. Lieut. Commander Baird could be called the "Adam of the Movement", as his work at the Base dated as far back as the Munich Crisis.

Captain Champion, replying to the toast, spoke of the solid foundation made by Captain Alison, upon which the Thames Naval Control had been constructed. He referred to the growth of the Base from the first authorised complement of but twelve officers, and of the three original officers still attached, namely, Payr. Lieut. Commander Baird, Lieut. Commander Braithwaite and Lieut. Commander Sandells. Much amusement was caused by the Captain's statement that the original room for operations in the Palace Hotel was later used by Commander Fox as a bedroom for 18 months. He went on to mention old friends who were now elsewhere, and those who had returned notably Captain Walley, who is with us again, and who was one of our first Commodores. He referred to the "thumping reputation" of the Base, and ended by thanking his staff, past and present, for their co-operation.

- 12 -

Lieut. Commander Braithwaite touched on the steady progress of the Thames Naval Control from the day after war was declared, and the birth of the A.A. Regt. when he was telephoned by the Duty Commander in the middle of the night, to be asked what he should do with a lorry and some 20 "something" Canadian soldiers who had suddenly made an appearance! He mentioned the untiring energy of Captain Alison (the first N.C.S.O.), and of Captain Hay, particularly the sound foundation of the Pier Head organisation, which still bore his mark. Numerous trials had been encountered and overcome since 1939. The Dunkirk activities was one of the most outstanding. The First Lieutenant ended on the note of the "Happy Ship". The Thames Naval Control was a "Happy Ship" principally due to the enthusiasm and untiring efforts of our Captain. He mentioned the work and popularity of Captain Goff during the few months he was N.C.S.O., then learning of his departure, the apprehension felt by all, and later the joy to learn of the return of Captain Champion. The following extract from a letter written by one of our Convoy Signalmen who had been wounded and invalided out, gave point to the First Lieutenant's theme:

> "I think the spirit that is fostered in the Navy is just about the grandest thing in the whole world. I learnt more about comradeship and good team spirit whilst I was in the service than ever before in my life, and know it will stay with me for the rest of my days......... I feel very proud that I have served with the Navy and I would give my ears to be back with you again. Those were the great days!"

Payr. Lieut. Commander Baird, after laughingly referring to one of the Chairman's remarks, dwelt on the contribution which had been made to the success of the Thames Naval Control by its first N.C.S.O., Captain Roger Alison. In war he was only with us for eight short hectic weeks, during which time the first Convoys were sailed, and the sure foundations of the Thames Naval Control structure laid. But this was only possible because of the study and preparations made by him in those fateful months between the Munich Crisis and the outbreak of the war.

Commander Rutley paid the stout-hearted men manning our Merchant Ships, to whom we all owe so much, a most sincere tribute

Commander Fox referred to the reputation of his temper and to the specially reinforced pipe presented by Pier Head which could not be bitten in half, however cross he might

- 13 -

become. He was followed by Captain Dane (R.N.O. Burnham), Lieut. Coxon, Payr. Lieut. Commander Stewart, Lieut. Burt, Surgeon Lieut. Paton and Major Lyttleton of the Mar. A.A. Regt. Lieut. Wilkins enacted his dive-bombing impersonation in his notorious French Captain interview.

The design on the menu card executed by Lieut. Pitcher contributed to the atmosphere of the proceedings, as this depicted a convoy at sea.

During the evening the Captain received and read the following telegram:-

"Your officers and ship's company tender their sincerest felicitations to you on the successful attainment of the first Southend Convoy Millenium."

A congratulatory message was also received from Captain Goff.

The room was suitably decorated with Flags representing the following signals:-

"N.C.S.O., Movement well executed. Go right ahead."

DO NOT PASS TOO CLOSE TO OTHER SHIPS FLYING BALLOONS.

IF YOUR BALLOON BECOMES UNMANAGABLE .... DEFLATE IT !!

- 14 -

By Yeoman L. F. Matthews.

Until we actually blew up, my thirty-ninth convoy had been, contrary to expectations, peaceful. The journey north had been very eventful. The night had been full of incidents, the longest bombing attack I have experienced, seven hours continuously from eight o'clock in the evening. It was a real ripe do. However, we were undamaged despite one ten yard near miss, one other ship was damaged but our escorting destroyer shot a Jerry down.

I had four days at the other end which passed pleasantly enough in the usual manner, sleeping, resting and enjoying myself generally. After the conference on a bright mild morning, we went aboard a tug en route for another little pleasure trip.

The signal staff consisted of Norman Taylor, who was mined a little while back, Bert Gwilliam, just returned from 14 days' survivors' leave, Gunn, a rather dreamy eighteen year old individual from Tamworth on his first trip, and myself. Altogether we were a pretty tough crew. My repeating signalman, Bert Ransome was aboard a small Norwegian vessel.

We went aboard. The ship was the S.S.......... She was spacious and clean, presenting large deck space with an excellent bridge and really gave one the impression of having plenty of room in which to move. We weighed anchor and proceeded. The weather appeared very promising, the sea being calm but some haze. This thickened until we were forced to use our siren to keep in touch. I had fears that this would cause the whole convoy to anchor and as we were in deep water we did not want to do this unless forced. However, about 2030 we came out into clarity once again, to the pleasant clearness of a September twilight in the North Sea. I reckoned on things being uneventful that night, Jerry would save it up for us tomorrow, and so I turned in, lying on the settee in the 3rd Mate's cabin and I had a very fine night's rest.

I went on to the bridge on Thursday morning before breakfast to find that nothing of importance had occurred during the night; everything quiet, everything peaceful.

The day was uneventful, the weather perfect and I spent most of my time sunning myself. Food was good and altogether this ship was one of

- 18 -

the nicest I had been on.   The officers all spoke with a definite American accent;   the Captain was, I think, originally a Cornishman and all three mates were very nice young fellows.

About tea-time we were getting near to what is known   as   "E-boat alley", the danger spot of the East Coast.   The night was bright and clear. I stayed aloft until gone midnight. Everybody was on the   qui vive   for attack.   The destroyers stood out starkly in the moonlight. Gunners stood with their fingers on the triggers.   Throughout the whole convoy number-less heroes in Duffel Coats with their tin hats ready to hand were strain-ing their eyes aloft and around ready for any attack from whatever quarter or by any means the enemy would employ.   However, it was not to be.   The night passed without any untoward incidents and with the dawn, wearied men turned in.   I however, had gone down soon after midnight as I sensed there would be nothing that night.

We were by now well down the coast - our destination was in sight. By early afternoon we should be near that cheerful place which has caused many of our hearts to lighten with relief upon sighting the lengthy pier. I was still faintly uneasy about this trip, notwithstanding the excellence of the ship and the nearness of our final destination.

About 1035 I told the signalmen to keep a lookout as I was going below.   I went into the saloon to sign the victualling forms, etc.   At 1043 we struck a mine amidships. With a tremendous explosion we heeled to port and I was thrown across the saloon, the lights of course went out and I could hear the crashing of the glassware and crockery. I quickly crawled to the starboard door which I succeeded in pushing open and got into the pantry. From there another door led on to the deck. I gained this through dust, steam and smoke and groping my way through this blinding atmosphere I found the starboard bridge ladder.

The siren had evidently jammed, for about the first minute. it kept up its weird and terrible sound. The death knell of the doomed ship.

I succeeded in climbing to the lower bridge and from thence attained the bridge. The starboard side on which I had so recently been standing and where I had left my Duffel Coat, cigarettes, life jacket etc. was cov-ered with a mass of debris. The wheelhouse, surrounding sand-bags, mortar blocks etc., had collapsed, covering it entirely.   By this time the smoke and dust were clearing.   I supposed that about 40 seconds had elapsed since we struck.   Number 4 hold in which was stored turps and resin was ablaze. All the life-boats were staved in. The ship was going rapidly under our feet.   One could feel her downward motion.

I managed to extricate my life jacket which I donned and to get my hand into my Duffel Coat pocket and extract my diary, that important piece of my kit.

- 19 -

The Pilot was the only man left on the bridge. He was very cool. He slung his gas mask and locked his case quite calmly. Going over to starboard and looking aft I saw my signalmen and one or two of the crew all rather dazed, standing on the lower bridge. By this time scalded and wounded men were crawling up from the stoke hole and there were some ghastly sights. I told Taylor to see what kit he could salvage whilst I went to the ruins of the wheelhouse and extricated the Confidential Book Bag which also had a revolver and one pair of binoculars inside. Looking around rapidly I saw that we could not save much more of our gear. It was mostly smashed, and besides, we did not have time.

Seeing that the boats were useless an attempt was being made to lower the port lower bridge jolly boat. I told the signalmen not to get in, which as it turned out, was a wise decision as she was overcrowded. Slipping down from the davits it partly turned over shooting men into the water in all directions. The Captain shouted, "Let's try the starboard side." A little group of us moved quickly over. I suppose two minutes had by now elapsed from the time she actually struck; the water was rising rapidly. The gunwhales were almost awash. Her 4.7" gun aft stuck grotesquely into the air where it had been forced from its mountings by the explosion. She had cracked amidships and the boilers were bursting as the salt water entered them.

We let go the starboard jolly boat which slid down at an angle, hitting the water with her forward end and getting swamped. I told Gwilliam and Gunn to drop into her and one or two others did likewise. By this time, the Captain, Pilot and myself appeared to be the only ones aboard and the Skipper ordered us both to drop into the boat which we did accordingly. We then pushed off but owing to being overcrowded and waterlogged we could not make headway and things were very uncomfortable.

When we were about ten yards off I saw Norman Taylor just scrambling out of the saloon loaded with gear, our gas masks over his shoulder. I shouted to him to drop the gear and run forward, which he did. By this time amidships was awash; No. 4 hold well alight and as her after end was going down the foredeck rose from the water. Taylor was joined by a wounded stoker, blood streaming from a gash on his head. They ran well forward and I shouted for them to jump. With their boots on they did so, and after desperate attempts we managed to haul them half into our waterlogged craft. I had an injured man across my knees and was supporting a sixty year old gunner in the water with my left arm. We were now so overcrowded that we had to jettison the oars, it was impossible to row.

I suppose that it was about $3\frac{1}{2}$ minutes from the time she struck until I left her, so it will be seen that she went pretty quickly.

The sea was covered with burning oil. Bales of cotton were being forced out of the gap in her side. Gurgles and explosions were coming from her. The funnel, after end, masts and foredeck were still above water. She began to settle and soon these had almost disappeared. She finally rested

- 20 -

75

on the sandy bottom, the top of her funnel and mast with the Commodore's pendant still gaily flying, being just above water.

We paddled toward a destroyer which was standing off and succeeded in getting near to her When alongside the overburdened little boat finally foundered but most of us managed to grasp the ropes which were trailing over her gunwhales. I grasped one with my right hand and supporting an injured man with my left, it was seconds only before brawny matelots hauled us aboard. This was accomplished at 1101.

The Captain, I was pleased to note was also saved. He jumped overboard from the port side with a badly scalded Lascar, and an officer from the destroyer dived overboard with a line and aided them both aboard. Men had been in the water all around, their heads bobbing above the surface. Luckily it was quite calm and they were, I believe, all picked up.

On board the destroyer were some twenty-six men. One that we had brought in, the Chief Engineer, was covered in oil fuel and was dead. Three others were badly wounded. Others of the crew had been picked up by motor launches and I do not think that out of the fifty-six men on board the ill-fated ship more than twelve were lost.

We were a motley crowd in various stages of undress, swigging rum and smoking cigarettes. We had clothing given us and finally, when it was clear that there were no more survivors we proceeded at full speed into port. The wounded were taken ashore by motor launch and later a tug landed us, which would be at about 2.30 in the afternoon.

After seeing the Jontie we were quickly away, dirty and dishevelled, travelling back by train to our Base. I made a couple of 'phone calls to reassure everyone as to our safety.

Less than fifty hours later on the 21st September, I was married and the 21 days' survivors' leave which I had been given naturally was very acceptable. The whole experience seems like a nightmare when I look back on it but it is surprising in a crisis how coolly one can take things. There were fine examples of courage and heroism. The whole affair was very sudden and as such was not so nerve-racking as some of my previous experiences while engaged on convoy work. However, I have no wish for it to be repeated.

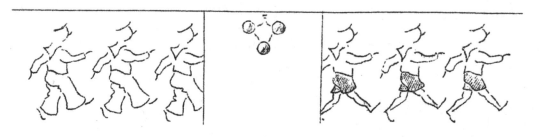

the pace rather against his wish.   Lieut. Plumb 23, O.Sig. Puddephat 20 and L.Sig. Nottage 29, helped Dutton in turn.   A few glasses of sherbert water and a few yarns at the Yacht Club afterward rounded off an enjoyable day.

Our last game to date was against Leigh Hall College, who put us in to bat.   We declared at 159 for 6, Naylor being very unlucky in missing his 50, being caught at 49.   Griffiths survived two or three chances to make 51.   The College were left two hours to get what we had made in $1\frac{3}{4}$ hours.   We had some early successes but when stumps were drawn we had only disposed of 6 wickets for 116 runs.

We have had to cancel one or two games being unable to raise a side owing to the exigencies of the service.   So far in nine games we have been represented by over 40 different officers and ratings.

Two local residents, through the War Efforts Committee, have kindly presented the Base with a bat, autographed by the last New Zealand touring side and also a set of stumps, for which suitable acknowledgment has been sent.

TENNIS.

The use of the Thorpe Bay Tennis Club has been very kindly offered to officers,   ratings and W.R.N.S. attached to this Base.   There are five hard courts and eleven grass courts.   Miss Royle, 21 Thorpe Bay Gardens, (Tel. 8721) would be very pleased to assist in arranging games, matches etc.

Considerable use has been made of this kind offer, and some excellent tennis has been enjoyed.

A friendly game with six members of the R.A.F. was played at Thorpe Bay on Tuesday, 7th July.   We lost 6 - 3, Roper and Turner being our most successful players.   Those taking part reported a thoroughly enjoyable time was had by all.   Miss Royle of the Thorpe Bay Tennis Club contributed in no small way to the success of the event.

Signal sent to Headquarters by Field Telephone:

"We are going to advance, can you send us reinforcements?"

Signal received:

"We are going to a dance, can you lend us three and fourpence?"

A MORNING IN THE CYPHER OFFICE

By a Newcomer.

0829.　Suddenly realise am on duty at 0830. Swallow last piece of toast whole, and grabbing gas mask etc., rush out of front door.　Try to run with dignity.　Arrive at Base, rush upstairs and collapse fainting in doorway of office.　Observe that clock says 0827, and the officer have come to relieve says, "How frightfully punctual you are." Try to explain about clocks, but find it too exhausting.　Ask if she had a good night.

Notice she looks slightly haggard, which not altogether surprising when she reveals that 6000 -----s arrived at 2300 and that she has been unravelling them ever since. Feel profound sympathy and say so.　Say hope she will have a good sleep. She says she hopes so too, and oh by the way before she goes she <u>must</u> tell me that OPS want six copies of the ----------. Write this down and pin in prominent position, as know to cost that memory seldom reliable. Mention that there is sardines on toast for breakfast.　She groans and says that'll mean she has nothing to eat all day be-

SLIGHTLY HAGGARD.

cause she'll miss lunch anyway, being asleep.　She says she can't <u>think</u> of anything to tell me, she <u>hopes</u> she hasn't forgotten anything, and <u>leaves</u>. Am left feeling that some people really do have Raw Deal.　Remember that am on to-night myself, so must not be too lavish with sympathy. Drag thoughts back to present and look through logs.　Read paper. Start guiltily as door opens; rush to cupboard and rustle papers as cannot get rid of idea that must always be doing <u>something</u>, even when nothing to do. Relapse into chair as messenger leaves and resume paper.

"TOO FRIGHTFUL FOR WORDS"

0900.　Door opens and Ravishing Creature wafts in; goes over to mirror and powders nose. Says, "How <u>simply</u> too frightful for <u>words</u> I look," and <u>wafts</u> out again. Reflect that some people are never satisfied and start crossword in paper.

0915.　Can only think of two words in cross-word and throw away in disgust.　Wonder if worth starting knitting.

0917.　'Phone rings and heart springs mouth-wards, as remember all things have done wrong during past 24 hours. Can hardly lift 'phone for shaking of hand, and relief almost un-bearable when voice of fellow officer says how is the biscuit situation, because if it's low she'll get some more. Say well actually

- 29 -

Night Watch finished them and no wonder. T/P girl enters with signal and says did I really mean this to go to NAA as she thinks the First Lieut. usually has it. Say yes of course she is quite right, he does, and wonder why born with very inferior ersatz brain. Depressing thought.

0920. Senior Cypher Officer enters and says she simply must look through logs as she hasn't done so for weeks. Clearly remember her doing so all previous afternoon but do not say so. Sharpen pencils. Become aware of heated conversation going on behind me, though no third person in room. Realise with a start that this is S.C.O. addressing logs.

0940 - 1015. Slight flow of activity far too secret to mention.

1015. 'Phone rings and am overwhelmed by paralysing sensation once more especially as definitely OPS line. Try to conceal utter horror and mouth into 'phone. OPS says will I confirm Very Peculiar Word he has found in his copy of recent signal. Confirm that word definitely wrong and send for miscreant. Says she is terribly sorry but fact is she is getting married next week, and - well, she doesn't seem to be able to keep mind on work. Feel this to be entirely reasonable. S.C.O. says fancy letting it affect you like that, and immediately relapses into reverie lasting about ten minutes, from which she emerges with the remark that if he can't get down this weekend she really will go Potty. Sympathise.

1030. Welcome sight in shape of messenger with tea. Am just about to drink when T/P girl announces that both machines have secret signal coming through. Rush to attend to it and by time finished with, find messenger with look of terrible reproach saying that my tea is COLD. Feel incredibly guilty, reflect on trouble of making, waste in war-time etc., and drink at one gulp.

1040. Signal Officer walks in, picks up nearest signal, scrutinizes closely and says, "Sent this all wrong of course, ----- fools." Exchanges raillery with S.C.O. Minor earthquake and in walks another C.O. with bags under each arm, saying, "Do have a biscuit everybody." Everybody does. Signal Officer says, "How are the fifteen brothers?" More raillery. Am called away, and return to see Signal Officer leaving with remark that something was a dirty crack. Wonder what.

DO HAVE A BISCUIT EVERYBODY

1100. Second C.O. leaves, having freely distributed biscuits, buns and chocolate, and given brief resume of proposed visit to town, involving meetings with boy friends too numerous to mention. Hear much chaff next door, followed by loud shrieks of laughter. Feel sorry to have missed Gems of Wit. S.C.O. says what was I thinking of when I gave the ---- ---- to CON. Say quite truthfully that cannot imagine. Wonder where thoughts are half the time.

1115.   Door opens and am confronted by duty officer; sheer undiluted horror sweeps over me as realise have done something too bad to say over 'phone. Functions of mind temporarily sus-
pended, but recover mental conscious-
ness in time to realise that All is Not Lost. D.O. obviously trying to explain nature of various papers he is holding, and giving instructions regarding same. Say do I understand? Say yes perfectly, as cannot bear to ask for repetition. Fortunately S.C.O. comes to rescue and Nation's fate is saved.   Am relieved as door closes.

AM CONFRONTED BY DUTY OFFICER

1116.   S.C.O. says, "Have a bun." Have one.

1117.   S.C.O. says, "Have a biscuit." Have one.

1118.   S.C.O. says, "Have a bit of chocolate."   Have one.

1130.   Receive signal to send to eleven places. Tell T/P girl who takes it very well.   Wonder how they manage to conceal feelings so cleverly.

1145.   Mysterious signal marked IMMEDIATE and URGENT arrives. Ask S.C.O. distribution. She says she thinks NC, OP, CON, RO, PHC, but isn't sure about DELS. I better go down and show OPS. I say couldn't, I'd 'phone. She says no, too long and secret. Realise no hope for it, and go down to OPS. Open door and receive confused impression of thick, thick fog, several wraith-like shapes, (which impression discover superficial when bump into one), and hive-like drone of voices. Wonder which direction to make for. Finally think discern outline of Duty Commander far away in distance, and make bee-line for. Am relieved to find am right.   Produce signal with feeling of triumph and ask What He Thinks About It. He glances at it and says not really of the slightest importance to anybody. Feel dashed and creep out, colliding with ghost as do so, atmosphere being of pea-soup denseness.   Wonder why always least important things marked "IMMEDIATE." Return to find S.C.O. singing "I can-not find it ANYWHERE" in rich con-
tralto. When venture to ask what, am informed red pencil missing, and both of us hunt for five minutes.   Finally, on happening to glance in mirror, she observes it in breast pocket and All Well.

1200.   First of eleven places comes through.

1210.   Both 'phones ring simultaneously.   Try to check rising feeling of panic and tell self must break self of habit. Pick up 'phones. One says

- 31 -

will I bring her case over when I come as she's left her slippers in it
and can't go to bed till arrives, the other says he thought he told me that
OPS wanted six copies of the ---- ----.   Tell them both (simultaneously)
to wait a minute and break out in cold sweat as realise destroyed piece of
paper about six copies in sudden tidiness campaign.   Tell one I will certainly bring it, and the other, I am very, very sorry, I can't think how
it happened, and collapse from nervous exhaustion. S.C.O. says, "Did they
want anything?"   Say oh no, it was just some little thing I forgot.   Rush
to typewriter and try to pretend am typing for practice.

1230.   Second place comes through.

1245.   S.C.O. says well, she really has looked through all the logs now,
she doesn't think there can be anything else to do, and goes.

1250.   Three signals arrive for despatch (eight places each).   At the
same time a string of four secrets appear.   Have just started second, when
T/P girl announces with triumph that can now get Broadcast to four places.
Rush out to take advantage of this.   Am in middle when fifth place appears
on other machine.   T/P girls keep it quiet by telling it frantically to
QQ whenever it shows signs of restlessness.   Finish Broadcast and rush to
find it on point of clearing.   Manage to pacify and sigh with relief when
signal despatched, but this tempered with fury when realise could have sent
other two signals off on Broadcast and will now have to get places all over
again.

1315.   Rush backwards and forwards from typewriter to teleprinter.   Every
thing hazy and confused.   Nine places come through at once, four on one
machine and five on the other.   In midst of haze have impression of Ravishing Creature floating in again saying, "My dear, I simply can't do anything with my hair, it looks simply too ghastly," but may be only mirage.

1335.   Emerge from debris to see relief sitting at typewriter.   Wonder
how she got there.   Suddenly notice all signals despatched.   Commence
mopping up operations.

1350.   All miraculously clear.   Practically no signs of former havoc!!
Feel as if had just emerged from anaesthetic after long and   harrowing
operation.   Realise only thought is lunch.   Wonder why rush hour always
at meal-times.   As limp out of office, hear relief say she hopes it will
be a Really Busy afternoon, they are much more fun.   Can   only   wonder
silently ....

- 32 -

There are 5 OBE's listed in this edition's Honours and Awards plus a Distinguished Service Medal for Convoy Leading Signalman W. E. J. Holm and many Mentioned in Despatches.

"MINES WERE LAID IN ENEMY WATERS" is an account by the well known NCS officer Commander L. Newman, RNR. Commander Newman in pages 3 – 7 gives his account of accompanying RAF bombers in mining the waters around Heligoland where there was German shipping.

According to page 8 Wrens were smitten by Southend Signalmen as described in the rhyme entitled "A Song of The Southend Signalmen".

We are all familiar with Rudyard Kipling's poem 'IF'. Here on page 16 is a different version by Charles Page. It is an NCS 'IF' with apologies to Rudyard Kipling.

Many Spun Yarn pages were dedicated to theatre productions performed at The Club with copy scripts printed showing the names of participants often including senior officer actors. Therefore it seems appropriate to print here just one of them. Pages 23 - 26 was a Revue entitled "Bends and Hitches" played to packed houses on 12th and 14th July 1943.

The following extract from page 29 is a Limerick appearing under the title "Nautical Smiles".

There's a place that's called Westcliff-on-Sea;

A paradox, quite, seems to me.

For its Cliffs have "gone West";

And as for the rest,

There is mud where the sea ought to be.

Honours and Awards.

The following officers and ratings have been decorated in the New Year and Birthday Honours Lists:-

ORDER OF THE BRITISH EMPIRE (MILITARY DIVISION)
Cdr.J.F.C.Bartley,D.S.C.,R.N.R. Cdr.A.H.Dyer,R.N.R.
Cdr.C.E.N.Frankcom,R.D.,R.N.R. Cdr.H.R.Lane,R.D.,R.N.R.
Cdr.E.R.Taylor,R.D.,R.N.R.

DISTINGUISHED SERVICE MEDAL
Convoy Leading Signalman W.E.J.Holm.

MENTIONED IN DESPATCHES
Cdr. F.A.G.Hunter,R.D.,R.N.R. Cdr. H.E.Morison,R.D.,R.N.R.
Convoy Ldg.Sig.H.G.Chamberlayne. Convoy Ldg.Sig.F.Eldred.
Convoy Ldg.Sig.F.Ireland. Convoy Ldg.Sig.B.Osborne.
Convoy Sig.W.Donald. Convoy Sig.H.H.Dutton.
Convoy Sig.G.Lloyd. 3/0 A.Coningham, W.R.N.S.

CONGRATULATIONS
to the following ratings and W.R.N.S. who have passed their officer's course:-

Con.Ldg.Sig.(now Sub.Lt.) B.H.Sayer. A.B.(now Sub.Lt.) S.M.Nunn.
Con.Sig.(now Sub.Lt.) J.E.Earl. Con.Sig.(now Sub.Lt.)Maldwyn Jones.
Con.Sig.(now Sub.Lt.) Maurice Jones. Con.Sig.(now Sub.Lt.) B.V.Lagrue.
Con.Sig.(now Sub.Lt.) A.M.Roper. Writer(now Pay.Sub.Lt.) F.Moody.
Con.Sig.(now Sub.Lt.) A.J.P.Puddephatt.
P.O.Wren(now 3rd.Officer) D.G.Fielding.
Ldg.Wren(now 3rd.Officer) O.M.Denman.
Wren (now 3rd.Officer) N.Corbett.

------oOoOooo------

- 2 -

MINES WERE LAID IN ENEMY WATERS.

by Cdr. L. Newman R.N.R.

"Last night a force of our Bombers raided occupied territory and mines were laid in enemy waters".

Such an announcement, now full of significance to me after my own experiences, is often received with a casual indifference as if it was little to do with our business. Bombing and so forth is the job of the R.A.F. Their organisation and intended schemes to get at the Hun is a closed book until the effort is made. To me, like a book of gripping interest, there are salient features indelibly impressed, which on closing the covers, only serve to seal their impression in fresh keeping.

My job was to carry the story of the Red Ensign to the Bomber crews and their station personnel, primarily as liaison and then to give topical interest to our own side of the War. I have been no little embarrassed and amazed by the accummulation of bouquets handed back to me for the "Dead End Kids" and our North Sea Coasters; I would like to take this chance of passing them on.

The boot, we feel, is on the other foot, and that our job is a pleasure trip in comparison with a night bomber at work.

Compliments and platitudes aside, I was soon inveigled by their laconic attitude to participate in a mine-laying trip over Heligoland, after all that was the natural result of mixing with airmen especially when their names are public legend. I have now flown with a V.C. (decorated since our trip together) which to me somehow puts a halo on things uneventful to him. A trip in another bomber over St. Nazaire proved much more exciting.

The weather grounded the mine-laying trip for three days and I was busy at other stations, when the news reached me that it was "Laid on".....

- 3 -

The Flight Officer's small vans were busy parking the crews at their aircraft dispersed widely around perimeter. These lads were all rigged for the job and it is next to impossible to walk in the clobber especially the fore, upper and rear gunners in their electrically heated leather suits and boots, harness, Mae West, and oxygen helmets. It was an hour before take off and I visualised at least half that time being required to transform me from a sailor to an airman; not so - an overall suit to keep me clean; next the flotation Mae West, parachute harness and helmet. Willing helpers togged me up rather like a horse is harnessed for speed at a fire station: "bit tight between the legs" - "Oh! that's all the better - be comfy when you're sitting down!" - "Yes, when" thought I. A Wing Commander Dortmund Ems fame drove me to the plane, the Squadron Leader piloting her (whom I had met previously) awaited my arrival- his crew at their posts inside already. There were ten minutes to spare, (time for the soothing weed which I had left behind) however, there was time for something else and standing in that harness!.......

I have now crawled along the inside of this giant Lancaster, it is her maiden Ops. trip (smell like a submarine) and sit athwart with her Captain with an array of instruments that later shimmer and shimmer before me luminously in the dark. "Contact" -one of four great engines, (they would start the one nearest me first!.) - a sheet of flame from the exhaust and the panel dash board dances on it's springs. I have meantime been locating the plug for the "Inter-com" which is surprisingly clear over the din outside. There is no need for the oxygen supply this trip and I mentally pledge myself that experience at a later date. I am handed a supply of chewing gum and chocolate, all four engines are now ticking over, warming up, no turning back now or changing my mind!

Dusk outside, exhaust pipes, glowing a cherry red which later becomes white (a sickening exposure like a ship in convoy having a funnel afire in E-Boat alley). Other machines which fascinated my attention throughout have taxied to the flare path, the Squadron Leader does not necessarily take off first nor do we arrive over the target in that order The full engine test, off brakes and taxying to the approach we join one of the two queues which have formed from outlying dispersal points, I have now developed a gloating thrill over the novelty of being at the delivery end of H.E., with the Hun, instead of receiving it. The first aircraft rears off down the flare path, and the second turns into position ere the first is airborne, the controller regulating ground movements by a green or red Aldis light. Our intercom is humming with comments from front gunner "G for George" air-

- 4 -

borne, "H for Harry next" that's us - I note the time and the straight line of runway lighting (like an eternally long street).Someone whistles a few bars - "switch off your mike Nobby" -from the pilot. I watch his right hand moving the four throttles in one movement and literally feel the thousands of horse power eclipse all other sensation. Speed over the ground seems infernally slow - I feel the presence of our cargo glueing us to the ground - 8 men and several times more H.E. than the early Hampden or Wimpy could carry.

The flare path lights are flickering by-at last our tail is up and we gather speed on two wheels more rapidly; red lights on hangers and perimeter heads, pilot is wholly engaged keeping her straight and level, an eternity seems passed before he eases us off and also the ten -sion which all must have felt. This is our first operational flight in this type of machine and the christening take off by all was successful. One hand now free from the controls the pilot operates undercarriage with lever by my left leg and concentrates on the fascinating adjustment of engine revs and the airscrews to coarse pitch.

Heat inside is terrific from the long take off burst,temperature outside 10°C,there is still a little daylight left and roads and rivers are discernable.The drome lighting is left astern after one circuit, we are climbing slowly on our course for the coast. I hope convoys will be well plotted as I have personally arranged for all aircraft to clear them on this flight. Intercom buzzes with pin points for navigator in which I join for the sheer novelty of using my mike.

Two other bombers are in sight as we cross the coast, right on track, later to fade into the obscurity of darkness, each independently navigated. This is a night well worth waiting for, clear,cloudless, a steady wind, sea disturbance from 2000 was last perceptible half an hour from the coast before swallowed by blackness which afforded no clue of what was beneath;during this transition stage the instrument panel slowly disappears leaving their luminous dials alone set out like rows of watches against a black velvet background. What is that in the sky ahead? Flare from a fire?a ship ablaze? No, just the moon!

- 5 -

Bomb doors are opened and closed to check satisfactory operation. We settle to comparative silence on the intercom and I begin to feel the grimness of the job, the white glows from the exhausts no longer alarm me and the moon has settled a serenity about the North Sea which I endeavour to assimilate with the help of chewing gum. My eyes are surely deceiving me now, the outer engine airscrew has stopped, no the exhaust is the same colour, oh!it's started again,slowly, like a lazy wind mill Gosh! it's gone from sight altogether. I look to the pressure gauges more to convince my eyes of their truth – again to the engine. There it is – the airscrew stock still and every two minutes the moonlight mag ic re-appears. Fascinating food for thought – brings me nearer to enemy territory without interior qualms or tummy rumbles which I had expected apparently I am viewing the outer airscrew through the disc formed by the inner one, which, revving slightly faster, causes the periodic illusory static. Remember cab wheels on the old"flicker" stopping and going astern.

There! a lone ship –must be the Hun Outer Patrol, in ten minutes we will see Heligoland. Temperature – C now, still warm inside and as light as day outside. Am expecting night fighter and flak, find I am standing up to get a clear all round view. Yes, there it is, flak a mile to the Southward.Broadcast this to all on the mike and forget to switch mine off –sounds like a number engaged and a broadcast reply,"switch off that b... mike" – realise it's mine and obey – must be getting excited. "That might be J. for Johnny" says someone in rather an abstract reply to my observation.

Think it prudent to shut up and not say any more – no – there it is surely! cannot resist it. Heligoland ahead on port bow sure enough – I can see ice on the shore and the island like a dark mist rising above it. Feel very bucked to have made a sensible remark and switch off mike properly. Hope pilot will alter course and shape for our pinpoint– not he!the navigator has to do that! no wonder this same pilot deserved

his V.C. three weeks later. On and on we stand skirting the island and leaving it astern – am wondering why the Hun is so quiet –not a gun or searchlight. Next, more ice and land and then the navigator uses his mike and round we come to 240° still at 2000 ft.Next "E.T.A.target 2245" that means that in another 5 minutes

– 6 –

we will be through with the job. Flak to South coming up from all directions. Have a detached feeling that I am glad it's someone else, but consider it no guarantee that it will not be our lot soon.We are losing height and that hand steals to the throttles and eases back – and back – ever so gently "265° for the run up Sir". A cold draught up my pants the bomb doors are open – the front gunner reports bomb doors open (he can see them hanging down from his glass house forward) 1,000 feet now 120 m.p.h. still losing height and speed. There is nothing but the sea below – the waves are still quite discernable in the moonlight 800-700 "stand by" – "steady" – one – (a slight shake and bump of the machine", 2,3,4,5,6,7,8,9,<u>one</u> (another bump) 2,3,4, etc, one again and so on, our cargo is dropped in penny numbers, 2,000 lbs at a time. The parting of each mine upsets our trim considerably and the pilot is hard put to it keeping straight and level so that our eggs are well and truly laid . Front gunner reports "bombs gone" and then "doors shut" as we make the last run up to Heligoland to check the position of our job,and the course for home.Then follows general distribution of chewing gum, chocolate and back chat over the intercom.

The final circuit and respectful silence as the night landing is made –will she ever touch down – the long row of dimmed lights race towards us at two miles a minute – a bump – then another – then we are down, brakes engage, we have landed at last. Whilst taxying to our isolated dispersal point,the pilot reports to control by R/T "H for Harry clear of flare path".All so simple when it's over. The cheery crowd of airmen assemble for interrogation by "Intelligence" –breakfast on bacon and eggs and so to bed in the early hours.

Such was my introduction to "mines were laid in enemy waters" – some of our bombers had drawn enemy flak,but to all (it appeared to me) just a trial run for these magnificent machines and an assessment of their performance for more strenuous jobs. We all know how these same Lancasters attacked Augsberg shortly afterwards; I was quite content to complete my picture with a night run to St.Nazaire and return fully satisfied with a sample of all the thrills and risks which our Whitleys (the early "contemptibles" of our bomber attacks) still endure after their long service.

– 7 –

1.

All you ladies of leisure,
I'll tell for your pleasure,
If attention to me you will lend,
An inspiring story
Of the valour and glory
Of the Signalmen bold of Southend.

2.

Though they're not very wealthy,
They're strong and they're healthy;
Their honour they'll fight to defend,
Only drafts give them pains,
Aches and varicose veins.
They prefer the soft airs of Southend.

3.

They are never dismayed
By the errors they've made;
As they go out to war with the Hun,
They joyously croon
Their signature tune,
"It's foolish but, by Heck, it is fun!"

4.

If a girl wants a sheik
Any day of the week,
And a man on whom to depend;
She cannot go wrong
If her choice is among
The Signalmen bold of Southend.

5.

If you ever get wrecked,
With no-one to protect
You, and life seems quite near to its end
Just take off your dress,
And hoist the distress,
Then wait for the men of Southend.

6.

If a poor little Wren
Thinks she's fallen again,
And behaves as though touched by the sun;
You can make a safe bet
That the fellow she's met
Is a bell bottomed Son of a Gun.

7.

If your wife's gone astray,
Or there's mines in the way
Of a convoy from here to Gravesend;
Just signal in haste
"There is no time to waste,
Please send us the Men of Southend."

8.

Oh, their famed versatility,
Noted ability,
Will soon bring this war to an end.
For they're dashing young seamen,
And regular he-men,
The Signalmen bold of Southend.

A Wren.

- 8 -

you can stay in OPS, aloof and placid,
When all around are wilting with the Strain.
If you can spend a day and night at PIER HEAD
And all the time your temper can retain.
If you can visit CONVOYS just at teatime,
And stay whilst all around you sit and drink
If you can ask the CYPHER OFFICE nicely
Why Secret Signal issued wasn't pink.

you can smile when C.B.'s come to muster
Your Confidential Books which are not there.
If you can subjugate all signs of fluster,
When Number One has raised a lively hare.
If you can spend an hour or two in ROUTEING
And calmly issue Chartlets by the score.
If PRINTING OFFICE finish countless Booklets
And you can ask them for a thousand more.

you can go to SICK BAY without flinching
And let the M.O. jab you with a knife.
If you can talk to ANC quite calmly,
When transfer rumours by the score are rife.
If you can answer questions by the dozen
The SEC might shoot at you from time to time.
And keep your head when K.B.O. informs you
That K.B's can't be disembarked at Tyne.

you can visit DEMS and talk of gunners
And not divert to tennis or to pubs.
And if Accountant O. should come towards you
Stand firm and unafraid of Wardroom subs.
If you can drive your efforts to the limit
Yet still make time for pleasure and for fun,
Yours is the Base and everything that's in it,
And what is more you'll beat the Hun my son!

- 16 -

THE THEATRE

"BENDS AND HITCHES". (St.John's Church Hall). 12th & 14th Jan.1943.

After seeing this Revue I wondered if someone had reminded the Braith Waits of Hilaire Belloc's truism,"There's nothing worth the wear of winning but laughter and the love of friends". An apt slogan for the Company certainly achieved these ambitions. Laughter is easy enough to win if you are content to let the audience laugh at you, but the Braith Waits succeeded in the hard way, for we laughed with them loud and long,

Which is more popular, Variety with its separate turns or non-stop Revue?. No answer here, for "Bends and Hitches" cleverly combined the two. Here we had a first half of Variety at its best, made possible by the polished compering of Payr.Lt.Cdr.Stewart,(there's only one Bill Stewart); the second half brought us into the realm of non-stop Revue, with slick cabaret turns following at fast pace.

The keen wit of William Barnacle(Lt.Cdr.Braithwaite), commenting on the audience without fear or favour, set a pace and a standard of novelty that was to continue throughout the show. His later appearance was even more anonymous. Cloaked in a mask of diabolical aspect, he became the solitary representative (apparently) of the staff of a vast night-club.In "Jack Takes Over", 3/O Pamela Digby-Bell and Sub.Lt.George Gibb combined with the Anchorettes,to put two vocal and dance routines over with great success. These two proved wonderful together as a team. We looked forward to seeing them again and were not disappointed, for they made a welcome re-appearance in the second half to sing to us again

The Anchorettes were one of the sensations of the show. Attractively dressed, they danced with the precision and lightness of welltrained chorines. I have never seen twelve Wrens look so happy in their work before, incidentally.

A sketch entitled "H.M.S. BLOWHARD" was very amusingly presented by Sub.Lt.Laurence, Ch.Yeo. Barrington, Sgt. Norton, R.M. Wren Allinson, L/Sig. Nottage, and Sig. Lawrence. A Wren Quartermaster

- 23 -

affected the audience very nearly as much as it did "Marine" Barrington. The age-old problem as to whether a beard should be worn inside or outside the bed clothes was solved by the "Commander" - it is worn on the forehead! "Cabin in the Cotton" provided a clever touch of contrast. Sweet and melodious, the harmonies of these Negro spirituals went straight to our hearts. 1st Officer Bowen-Jones who led these sweet singers, must have been gratified by their great reception. "Just a Hitch" was, as it's name applies, a quick black-out sketch (with a moral) well put over by Surg. Lt. McBain, Payr. Lt. Handley, 3/0 Echalez and Wren Evans. This was followed by Bessie William's Squad-drill Lovelies, who performed prodigies of drill-in-reverse in their novel and amusing way.

Betty Pearce did not belie the title of "The Navy's Sweetheart". "Salome" and "Maybe" were sung with the verve and personality which gave these two numbers maximum lift and expression. After this came ten minutes of fantastic craziness. Sub. Lt. Robinson as a conjuror inviting a mysterious Eastern potentate and his aide to witness his prowess from the stage, gives scope for almost anything. When the Rajah and his interpreter are none other than Surg. Lt. Cdr. Levy and Surg. Lt. McBain accompanied by a pantechnicon of props, then Reason becomes unsettled on her throne. A very hilarious ten minutes. The musical extravaganza "At the Overcliff Hotel" was an ingenious burlesque of the Overcliff Hotel's Night of Terror, danced and sung to the tune of "John Brown's Body". The first half was brought to a close by "Swingtime" a medley of numbers old and new presented by Sig. Freddie Brooks on his accordian. Riotous comedy was lent to this act by the two Dames, Sub. Lieuts. White and Gibb.

Part Two was gala night at the "Fo'castle Club", with it's attractive modern setting designed by Sig. Sturtevant and executed by the designer and Jnr. Skilling. 3/0 Digby-Bell and the Anchorettes gave the second half a stupendous start with their "Fleet's In" number. Payr. Lt. Cdr. Stewart then attempted, as an old-style entertainer, to put over "The Green Eye of the Little Yellow God". To the huge delight of the audience he was frustrated at every turn by two fierce looking Army Visitors to the Club, in the persons of Lt. Norman and Sub. Lt. Gibb. A very topical version of "You're the Tops" was sung by 3/0 Opal Echalez, and Lt. Henman. It was delightful and richly deserved the applause it received. The Westcliff Sisters (Peggy Whibley and Daphne Gavin-Jones) came next with a clever act of the type made so popular by the Western Brothers, and the audience were keen to appreciate the barbed shafts of sophistry which were so well put over.

The Russian Ballet was a complete contrast. Excellently done the colour, costumes, and lighting were most effective. Hilda Hornby was the ballerina of this exciting excerpt, with choreography by Noreen Carr. A new and likeable comedian was presented in L/Sig. Jack Courtney. Singing

- 24 -

catchy and amusing numbers, the act was enlivened by brisk and clever patter. The impressions of trumpet, harmonica, and guitar given by Sig. Mick Mott were amazingly faithful to the real instruments, while following him came A.B. Harry Kinnerman, to prove once again his complete mastery of the harmonica. His numbers were rendered with exquisite technique, and the applause was sensational.

The second half came to an end with the welcome re-appearance of Payr.Lt.Cdr.Stewart, this time with a colossal (in every respect) burlesque of Carmen Miranda. This was one of the high-spots of the programme, and left the audience in that perfect frame of mind - they were sorry it was all over. The cast of nearly seventy took their well deserved applause, and the curtain fell on a grand show. A big hand for Payr.Lt.Handley as the post-card seller, seizing his opportunities with masterly timing. The musical side was expertly handled by the R.A.F.Orchestra directed by Band Cpl. Miles. Accompaniment to some of the numbers and at rehearsals was by L/Sig. Ken Wheeley, for whose time and trouble both cast and subsequently audience must be indebted. To the smooth and slick production all credit must be given to L/Sig. Norman Hamill, the stage manager, and his assistants Sigs. Hales, Whittaker, Roddis, Dennis and Donald. Lighting was carried out by P.O. Tel. Lohden and operated by Tel. Honey. Decor by Sig. Sturtevant and erected by Jnr. Skilling. Crowded performances threw added responsibility to the House Manager, L/Sig. Nottage, with which he dealt with tact and efficiency.

I have deliberately left until the last the founder of this theatrical feast. That a "Ships Concert" blossomed into the full flower of revue was primarily due to Payr.Sub.Lieut. Milnes, producer-cum-compere, who provided the necessary coat of polish and got a richly reserved curtain at both perform -ances.

"Bends and Hitches" subsequently went on tour on February 2nd. and 3rd. when it played to crowded houses at WEST- CLIFF, and it is satisfactory to report that the Show was equally successful in this more sophisticated atmosphere.

"SINBAD."

(continued on page 32)

- 25 -

93

- 26 -

See page 1 Editorial with comments by Gurney Braithwaite about paper shortage and reduced numbers printed for the previous edition. Also see Obituary of Commander Arthur William Legge, RNR.

Page 2 contains a rhyming poem entitled "Mersig" by contributor O.D. who offers apologies to Lewis Carroll. This page is a typical example of the use of text with cartoon drawings.

Page 18 headed "FUN AND GAMES" makes reference to the 'Barnacle Club', to which, in evidence of its name, the oldest NCS members belong. See cartoon faces of left to right Lieut. Commanders Baird, Gurney Braithwaite and Sandells.

Gurney Braithwaite MP's special "Beneath Big Ben" contribution on pages 20 - 22 gives a first-hand account of his attendance at The House of Commons as witness to one of Winston Churchill's greatest speeches. The Prime Minister spoke to a packed house captivating everyone at his most inspiring.

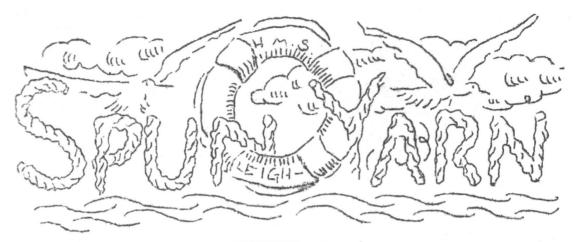

EDITORIAL.

The new "SPUN YARN" team is now well into its stride, this number appears punctually to schedule, and we shall hope to publish at four monthly intervals from now onwards. I must thank our lower deck contributors for the large amount of copy submitted - lack of space has forced us to pick and choose and many would-be poets must in consequence continue to blush unseen.

Congratulations to our prize-winners and for the unsuccessful there is always next time - in this case our edition of March 1944, when cash offers of the same amounts are again available.

Our last issue disappeared like hot cakes and I much regret that paper rationing limits us to five hundred copies. These are dispersed all over the world and it is pleasant to acknowledge appreciations from New York, Sierra Leone and Colombo.

J.G.B.

--------0--------

It is with deepest regret that we have to announce the death on October 3rd, following a short illness, of our shipmate, Lieutenant-Commander Arthur William Legge, R.N.R., who had served in the Convoy Department for the past two and a half years.

He was deservedly popular, both at the Base and among the Merchant Navy Officers with whom he came in contact at the many convoy conferences over which he presided. His kindness and geniality will be ever remembered by those who had the honour to work with this great gentleman.

--------0--------

by O.D.   (with apologies to Lewis Carroll)

T'was Mersig and the Ruddy Nore,
Did Cant and Barrow in the wave,
All rocky was the Commodore,
When the signal flags outrave.

Beware the Messerschmidt my son,
The guns that bark, the bombs that drop,
Beware the Heinkel one one ONE,
Avoid the place where E Boats stop.

And so, with Hotchkiss near to hand,
In Flamborough Dudgeon did he fret,
And with a port and starboard hand,
Clewed up another cigarette.

Expectorating thoughts aloud,
The Messerschmidt, with spurts of flame,
Came heiling through the Leaden cloud,
And achtunged as it came.

One strip! Two strip! from all the ships,
The retching guns spat death in morse,
They shot it down and saw it drown,
Then steaded on their course.

And hast thou slain the Messerschmidt?
Thou didst not join the stragglers club?
Oh this is jake, a piece of cake,
And likewise lovely grub.

T'was Mersig, still the Ruddy Nore,
Did Cant and Barrow in the wave,
More Rocky was the Commodore,
When the signal flags outrave.

- 2 -

Those who visit our Base from other ships and establishments often remark on the "family atmosphere" at Southend. It's certainly there all right and some family at that! For those who enjoy the social round there has been quite a lot doing since "SPUN YARN" last appeared in July.

For instance in all the best regulated families (and most ill-regulated ones, come to that) there is a wedding now and then. We haven't done too badly in that line ourselves. I was a guest at St.John's Church - and subsequently the "Royal" - at the marriage of Leading Signalman Williams and P.O. Wren Crofts on August 7th. This very popular pair of shipmates received a handsome present from the Convoy Signalmen. Then on the fourth

THE BASE'S 3 OLDEST OFFICERS

anniversary of the outbreak of War, September 3rd. the Captain was entertained to dinner by the "Barnacle Club", the three officers who have served at the Base right from the beginning - Lieutenant-Commanders Baird Braithwaite and Sandells. One can make no attempt to follow the course of this event except to record that the convoy assembled at the Alexandra Yacht Club and was subsequently seen tacking up the High Street.

With the coming of autumn our thoughts turn once again to the -room and the season had a smashing send-off on September 13th. when Ship's Club gave an invitation dance at the Queen's. All those who have befriended this excellent institution were among the company including the concert-parties who have given entertainments at the Church Hall. The Captain paid a welcome visit during the evening and the Club Committee desire to acknowledge four spot prizes, kindly given by a lady who insisted upon anonymity. Paymaster Lieutenant Milnes was his inimitable self as M.C. and our kind hosts can congratulate themselves on a first-class success.

- 18 -

Beneath Big Ben

Jimmy the one

History relates that one summer's morn in happier times a peer of
the realm, with a somewhat exaggerated idea of his own importance arriv -
ed in London to attend a sitting of the Upper House. Jumping into a taxi
at Paddington he barked the monosyllable "LORDS" to the driver and was
both surprised and indignant to find himself being rapidly driven in the
direction of St.John's Wood instead of Westminster.

No such misunderstanding is possible in the case of our elected
representatives so that when on Tuesday, September 21st. I boarded a taxi
in Fenchurch Street saying "COMMONS - MEMBERS ENTRANCE" my Jehu remarked
with Cockney nonchalance:-"Glad to see 'Is Nibs is back. Wonderful bloke
ain't he?". This observation nicely sums up opinion both inside and outside the House so that it was not surprising to find an almost 100% attendance to greet " 'Is Nibs" in the mood of restrained rejoicing which
the Englishman assumes when the news is good.

Just before Mr.Speaker entered for Prayers a shadow fell across
us as the news came through of the death of Sir Kingsley Wood, Chancellor
of the Exchequer since 1940, and a good House of Commons man. However important the occasion, questions to Ministers always occupy the first hour
of the day, thus upholding a historic tradition by which the ventilation
of grievances by private members must take precedence over Government
business. Sometimes a seemingly harmless question produces a small storm
and so it was on this occasion. A private soldier had been wrongfully
confined for eight days and nights in an unlighted and unheated cell. The
Secretary of State for War failed to satisfy the House that those respon
-sible had been adequately punished and soon found supplementary queries
pouring on him from all quarters. Eventually the Prime Minister's long-

- 20 -

awaited speech has held up for twenty minutes while attempts were made
to move the adjournment of the House. This incident gives an interesting
and valuable example of the power of a parliamentary democracy. Here was
a statement of world importance on tremendous military events delayed for
twenty minutes while the maltreatment of a quite unknown member of the
fighting rank and file was brought into the full light of day.

When Mr.Churchill eventually rose the House was packed as never
before in my recollection. It is not constructed to accommodate its full
complement of 615, and Members had to sit in the gangways and even, in
some cases, upon one another's knees, making the whole scene suggestive
of a Milnes burlesque of the Happy Valley in the gloaming of a June evening. Mr.Churchill was in his best form, looking much fitter for his Atlantic voyage.Confidently he strode through sheets of comforting statistics. The R.A.F. alone is now greater by 50% than the Luftwaffe- our aero
plane production is as 4 to 1 compared with Germany -in 1944 the bombing
of enemy buildings should reach "saturation point".

All this the House cheered and when the Prime Minister turned to
the "sea affair" he was no less encouraging. The sinking of U-boats goes
on apace - no ship has been lost in the North Atlantic for four months -
for the first fourteen days of September no Allied vessel had been sunk
anywhere throughout the Seven Seas - the gain of Allied merchant tonnage
in 1943 has up to date reached 6,000,000 tons and will soon have made
good all our losses since the outbreak of war. Then came a reference to
Japan, whose troops,no longer dying to the last man, have developed the
technique of "retirement according to plan". "They must be kept on the
run," said Winston, adding, as he thumped the dispatch box - "It's the
pace that kills!"

The circumstances surrounding the Italian Armistice and the escape
of Mussolini brought the first interruptions. Certain Socialist Members
objected to our negotiating with the Badoglio Government, which had sent
its fleet to Malta, and in many cases had troops fighting the Germans.
This brought down upon them the withering Churchillian retort:"Honourable
Members forget the importance of diminishing the burden which our soldiers have to bear. By this time it was half past one and the Premier was
halfway through his statement, so we took the unusual step of a luncheon
interval of one hour. On the resumption the speech reviewed future poss-
ibilities and dealt with the Second Front agitation. "We shall not be
forced or cajoled into undertaking vast operations of war against our
better judgment in order to gain political unanimity or a cheer from any
quarter". Relations with America, the need to maintain the blockade at
its fullest intensity despite the sufferings of the occupied countries,
the plight of the enemy satellite states Hungary, Roumania, Bulgaria and
a renewed declaration of faith in final victory brought Mr. Churchill's
speech to a majestic conclusion with a sweeping peroration which set the
House cheering for several minutes. Several contributions by back-bench-

- 21 -

100

ers f~llowed-but-there-is-always-committee-work-to-be-done and the House
soon emptied.

Comment everywhere was enthusiastic and optimistic;undoubtedly we
had been treated to "one of Winston's best". Before catching my train to
Southend there was time to attend the Serving Members' Committee, which
is an all-party group devoting itself to the problems which beset the
forces.

Passing down Whitehall everyone seemed to be carrying an evening
paper, heavily headlined with Churchillisms and in the tube all were an-
imatedly discussing the Premier's words. It was evident that he had- not
for the first time -administered a refreshing tonic to his fellow count-
rymen.We all seemed more confident and alert as the result of his return.
Yes = "Glad to see 'Im Nibs is back = wonderful bloke, ain't he?"

----------O----------

The F.S. Commodore was allotted a ship flying the flag of a gallant ally. The compass proved erratic and a check-up became desirable.

"Here comes the sun," said the Commodore, "please send down for
the azimuth."

The Officer of the Watch duly dispatched a Chit to do the necessary.

After a long delay this messenger returned to report-"The steward
says - sorry he's only got Manhattan."

----------O----------

REPORTER: "I've got a perfect new story."

EDITOR: "How come? Man bite a dog?"

REPORTER: "No, but a hydrant sprinkled one."

----------O----------

- 22 -

- SPUN-YARN -

The Journal of the Thames Naval Control.

★ ★

PRICE SIXPENCE ★ APRIL ★ 1944

Supplementary Sheet shows mini cartoon by Lieut. Charles Page RNVR inviting orders for larger sized copies. The drawings show his cartoon style which will be recognised in many of the Spun Yarn editions.

We may be familiar with MTB's and MGB's but perhaps not with ML's. Motor Launches were high speed military craft used by the navy. These "Small Ships" were engaged to protect harbours, to seek out U-boats and for air rescues. Pages 3 - 6 and bottom part of page 17 explain day to day life in an ML on a three day exercise. These busy little ships were just one of the many supporting craft for coastal operations and convoys.

Engagements and marriages were an inevitable consequence of 'boy meets girl' in wartime Southend. Details were regularly recorded in Spun Yarn editions. Page 19 is just one such record but I wish to draw attention to "BIRTHS". There are four recorded births. If any of those babies, now around 80 years of age, read this and have pictures or memorabilia from their parents time here I would love to hear from them. They are Brian Hugh Sturtevant, Derek Peter Spragg, Carol Lesley Holmes and Angela Helen Reynolds. Are you out there?

Pages 26 and 27 under the title "Fun and Games" record parties held at The Queens Hotel, The Clifton Hotel and the St. John's hall Southend Base Club. On page 27 is the farewell of Lieut. Commander Sir Joseph Gurney Braithwaite, 1st Baronet and MP who was No. 1 officer at NCS Southend from early 1941 until end of February 1944.

Page 28 is entitled "LINES WRITTEN IN COVENT GARDEN OPERA HOUSE" by Ralph Saunders Currie. I have no information on the origin of this piece but it is very funny.

Page 31 is pure 'Dad's Army' but at the time they were just known as the "HOME GUARD" which is what this hilarious piece is about.

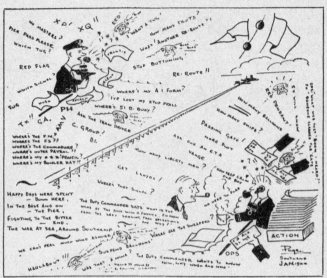

NAVAL "CONTROL"
NO   RUDDY . PANICO ! ! !

PRO BONO PUBLICO!

Alumnae of the Southend Base,
Recalling fast and furious pace
Pervading Ops. full round the clock,
May now perceive the flap en bloc.

Example small above is seen,
Too small to see the wit so keen,
Or even a Commander's rage,
Depicted by Lieutenant Page.

If you would have a thing to prize,
A cartoon of twelve times this size,
Peruse instructions writ below,
And quickly order 'fore they go!

---

*Copies of the above Cartoon by Lieut. Charles Page, R.N.V.R.,
size 14" by 12" and printed on Art Paper suitable for framing,
may be obtained from the Editor, "SPUN-YARN", c/o The
Accountant Officer, H.M. Naval Base Southend.
Price :— 6d. each.*

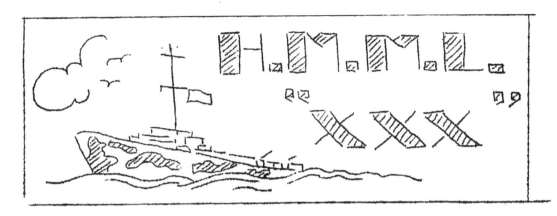

By:- F. L. Hogg.

"----- Our Light Coastal Forces engaged an enemy convoy off the French Coast in the early hours of this morning. Direct hits were scored on two enemy trawlers which were left in a sinking condition..."

Bulletins like this have become familiar to B. B. C. listeners, and many exciting tales have been recounted by the Officers and men who have taken part in these engagements at close quarters with the enemy. The offensive operations have added many more pages to the glorious history of the Royal Navy.

Sister ships to the M.T.B.'s and M.G.B.'s are the M.L.'s. Commanded in the majority of cases by young R.N.V.R., and occasionally R.N.R. officers, these Little Ships are on the job day in, day out, keeping an endless watch on our coast-line. The crew probably musters two officers and from fourteen to eighteen men. Most of them "H.O." ratings from all spheres of life, living and working together, and I can truly say I have never met a happier ship's company than that of H.M.M.L."XXX" whose story is related here.

The engine room staff consisted of "Taffy", a Petty Officer Motor Mechanic, and three stokers. Their's the duty to keep the powerful engines in perfect trim, and keep the engine-room as clean and as comfortable to work in as possible. Really a hard and nerve-racking job. The roar of the engines is so intense, that even the worst Bing Crosby can sing away without annoying his "Oppo". The remainder of the crew consisted of a "Sparks" and a number of seamen. By no means the least notable of these was Benjamin, a well-built, good humoured, and very willing Cockney lad, whose exploits kept the rest of the crew in a good humour from the word go.

Now meet the Skipper - a twentythree year-old R.N.R. two ringer, holding a D.S.C. and a "Mention", with two F.W.190's to his credit. Very popular with his crew, both for his ability and his untiring efforts to keep "XXX" a happy ship, (most necessary in the Little Ships where every man must know something of the other man's job).

-3-

0615 on a cold February morning finds our Base a hive of industry. The gentle hum of the engines indicates a final run-over by Taffy.
Ashore, still under the cover of the blackout, the Skipper receives his
final orders, to come back on board again and be greeted with .... an
appetising smell of grilling bacon, and coffee, turned out to almost the
perfection of a West-end chef - repeat "almost"!

Breakfast over, all hands turn to, and at 0730 in the grey dawn
of morning we are "in all respects ready for sea". The Skipper appears on
the bridge draped in muffler and sheepskin jacket......
"Okay Engine-room?...Okay Cox'n?...Let go for'd..Slow astern Starboard...
Ah! She's coming round beautifully......let go aft!......Okay No.1., look
after the decks and I'll stay on watch 'til we're clear".

With the light of morning slowly breaking through, we find ourselves in the open sea. Ropes and fenders are
stowed away, decks cleared, as we settle down
to sea routine which will be ours for three
days. The sea is inclined to be a little choppy,
and a biting wind makes quick work of reddening
our ears and noses. Hot cocoa from the galley
is always welcome, and appears on the bridge
about once an hour.

All goes well, as the sturdy little
craft ploughs her way carefully but surely through the waves - bent on relieving her sister
ship who has been keeping the last three days
patrol. Guns are being tested when we are well
clear, and all seems well when up pops Benjamin.
"Excuse me, Sir, but I've a jam with the Lewis!"
"What's all this?.......Why not try filling the pans with ammo, it would
probably make a big improvement!"
"Er...yessir, certainly, sir".
"Now for not using your loaf you can consider yourself duty "rolling chock
operator' for the rest of the trip".
"Yessir, certainly, very good sir!"
A lengthy explanation follows on how the bilge pumps should be manned
four times daily for half an hour each time. Benjamin "gets it" all right!

After four hours our sister ship is spotted on the horizon, and
greetings are exchanged by lamp. Weather reports follow, and when Service
matters are cleared up, further reports follow of a slightly more social
nature.....! Company parted at last, we set off on our patrol.

Shortly after lunch, Sparks rings through with ....From
N.O.I.C., sir. Floating mine sighted in vicinity of Z Buoy. Investigate
and take any action necessary".
"Right!....Cox'n, swing her round and steer Nor'West. Full ahead both,
and get all available hands on deck as look-outs. Take over No.1. while
I take a peep at the chart".

-4-

A few hurried calculations, a steady course, and soon our eager eyes make out Z Buoy on the horizon. Thoughts of a fish supper pass through our minds until the mine hove into sight. Keeping a safe distance away, the Skipper orders 'Action Stations' to be shortly followed by the order to open fire. Careful training of the Lewis brings its reward. A few seconds later there is a terrific explosion, the ship vibrates violently even at this distance, and a column of water is thrown up into the air .....then silence.

The "job" finished, and a report made, it now remains to wait about to collect the fish which have been stunned by the explosion and floated to the surface. Enough fresh fish for a week, with a corresponding reduction in the mess bill, is ample reward for the ship's company!

With Cook busy in the galley, and watch-below lending a hand in cleaning both guns and fish, we set off once again on our patrol. More cocoa is handed round and extra woollies are donned as the wind starts to freshen. We seem to be in for a rough time ahead. Oilskins follow as rain adds to our troubles, but the day is saved when Sparks reports, "Message from C-in-C, sir. Gale warning. Report to-----harbour forthwith". The Skipper takes her farther inshore to get a little protection from the wind, and we hug the coast like this until harbour is reached.

Once inside the harbour and safely berthed alongside an old coal barge, we settle down to our supper of fish, and discuss over the meal our chances of a night "in" if the gale continues. A signal is brought down with orders to remain at half an-hour's notice - quite promising - and as the night is yet young we content ourselves with listening to the radio and writing a few lines home.

Presently Benjamin taps on the Wardroom door, "Excuse me, sir but could we plug into the shore lighting?"
"It's a good idea, Benjamin, me lad, but we haven't any amps on board!"
"No amps, sir?, a little puzzled.
"That's right, Benjamin, no amps".
" Well, sir couldn't we get any ashore?"
'Mid cheers from the crew, he was last seen that night crossing the coal-barge and climbing a shaky rope ladder, complete with a bucket, "to collect a bucketful of amps for the shore lighting".

An early night seemed popular to get a few hours sleep. This was well worth while, for at 0315 came "Proceed to sea on normal patrol forthwith". The deck sentry was not received in great favour when he climbed below to call the duty watch. However half an hour later found us feeling our way out of the strange harbour - quite a tricky job on a very dark night.

Half an hour's run brought us to the channel which was to be the beginning of our patrol. Once on a steady course we slacken down, and soon feel ready for a snack. Hot dripping toast is the answer, and with this

-5-

107

inside us, we settle down to what we hope will prove to be a quiet night - although on the qui-vive for any emergency should it arise.

Hopes fulfilled, Dawn breaks with an atmosphere of peace. We report our position, and have a friendly chat by lamp with a lighthouse keeper. These lonely heroes, who keep watchful eyes on our shipping both in peace and in war, are used to our "Little Ships" passing their way up and down.

The wind has died down, the sea is calm, and that pleasant aroma once again arises from the galley... announcing breakfast.

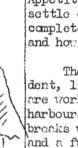

Appetites are satisfied, and once again we settle down to the morning's routine. This completed, at six bells comes "Up Spirits" - and how welcome on this biting cold morning!

The rest of the day passes without incident, likewise the night, though this time we are working it watch-about and no spell in harbour. So we are very thankful when dawn breaks with the prospect of being relieved and a further spell ashore. However the patrol is not over yet. On our trip back to harbour "Sparks" reports a signal, "Fighter Pilot brought down in the sea - investigate" together with a very approximate position.

Many have been saved by prompt action of the "Little Ships" in the past, and now seemed to be our chance too. At the order "Full ahead both", the little craft surges forward, guns manned ready for any enemy planes lurking round the scene of the disaster. On deck, all available hands are keeping a keen look-out for a sign of the pilot. With our estimated position reached and checked, there is no sign of wreckage or anything at all, and it now remains to start a search.

Ah! What's that?....three more M.L.'s coming up to join in the search. Over three hours pass, with hopes almost gone, when suddenly....
"Object bearing green nine-oh, sir!"
Glasses trained... all eyes anxiously cover the bearing indicated.
"Starboard twenty!" Quickly we alter course.
"Ease to ten.....'midships.....steady as you go"
Slowly we draw nearer and nearer, and then.....
"Yes! Its a rubber dinghy all right. The chap seems okay, he's waving to us!"

"Stop both... stand by to lend a hand for'd!"
A smiling lad of nineteen in the dinghy tells anxious enquirers he's Okay, 'cept for wind and wet. Odd jumpers, socks, pants, make a heterogeneous wardrobe at our survivor's disposal after a strip down and warm up at the Ward Room fire. A tot of "neaters" is forthcoming to complete the "cure".

-6-   Continued on Page 17.

Crawling away in retreat, I heard a lot of noise coming from the other side of the stairs, and found it pouring out of a room marked 'Ward Room'. Thinking it was now or never, I knocked a little belligerently, as I was beginning to get fed up with the whole business. Nothing happened of course, so pushing open the door, I looked in. There was a short officer rather like the furtive individual who had crept in earlier and who, judging by the excitement, was about to take his turn on the shove ha' penny board. Playing against him was another officer with one gold band, whereas the first had two, and I thought he must be higher up. No one took the slightest notice of me, they were all too intent on the game. The short officer took careful aim, and judging by the yells of derision, he lost. There were remarks about "visitors walking off with our half-crowns".

At this moment someone arrived and said something about the ship's company having fallen in for inspection. This seemed to be a signal for everyone to disappear, leaving me standing alone once more. Wandering downstairs, I found the resplendent cadet still there. I explained once more that I wanted to join.

"I'm afraid you are too late my lad. You must come early some other time. And in any case", he continued "We are having the Commodore's Inspection tonight, so buzz away out of sight till next Monday".

I went home...... but I was there early enough on the Monday all right! By the way, I have been in the Cadet Corps a month now, and confidentaally, now I know what it's all about, they are a grand lot !. All I have done so far is clean ship, but I still live in hopes something will happen, even yet!

--oOo--

H.M. MOTOR LAUNCH "XXX", continued from page 6.

A proud ship enters our home base on return from patrol. The crew in their smart sea-rig: white jumpers and bell-bottoms line the quarter deck to take the salute as we come alongside the quay. We tie up, our pilot friend is landed into the safe hands of the M.O., and we clean ship preparatory to a run ashore, At 1600, the job complete, ashore we go.

And thus we leave our "Little Ship", wishing her Godspeed whereever she goes, and happy landfall to all her gallant little crew. I have told you but a fraction of the many duties H.M.M.L. "XXX", will have to perform in the course of her career...lots of them boring, and yet many redolent with excitement and danger. Every day brings something new in the gallant work these ships are doing as the eyes of our coasts. Good luck to them all!

-17-

"SPUN YARN" GAZETTE. (Continued from page 2).

PROMOTIONS TO OFFICER:

To Acting Third Officer, W.R.N.S.:-

Wren I.F. BOUND.   Wren K.K. ORR.   Wren C.M. Phillips.   Wren J.A. GREGSON
        Ldg.Wren R. ORTON.   Wren O.M.D. BROMHALL.

.........oOo........

ENGAGEMENTS:

Lieut. F. L. HOGG, R.N.V.R. and P.O.Wren J. BLACKBURN....November, 1943.

Con.Ldg.Sig. K. J. WHEELEY and Wren V. ROBINSON.........December, 1943.

.........oOo........

MARRIAGES.

F/Lt. J. C. COX and Wren D. S. SAYERS .... 6th.December, 1943.

Con.Ldg.Sig. F. ELDRED and Wren H. E. MILLER ...... 28th.December, 1943.

P.O.Writer W. H. BODDY and Ldg.Wren D. KNIGHT...... 21st.February, 1944.

Sub.Lieut. O. G. WILLIS, R.N.V.R. and Miss. J. CHILCOTT, A.T.S........
                              16th.March, 1944.

Sub.Lieut. J. DEALEY, R.N.V.R. and 3/O M. E. MARSHALL, W.R.N.S..........
                              29th.March, 1944.

.........oOo........

BIRTHS:

To Con.Sig. A. STURTIVANT and Mrs. Sturtivant on 19th. August, 1943, a son, Brian Hugh.

To Con Ldg.Sig. H. SPRAGG and Mrs. Spragg, on 23rd. August, 1943, a son Derek Peter.

To Lieut. M. J. HOLMES, R.N.V.R. and Mrs. Holmes, on 13th. January 1944, a daughter, Carol Lesley.

To. A/B, B. J. REYNOLDS and Mrs. Reynolds, on 23rd. February, 1944 a daughter, Angela Helen.

.........oOo........

-19-

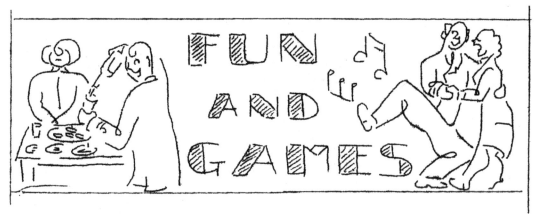

By:- "The Socialite"

Various sections of our community have managed to drive dull care away on suitable occasions during the Winter Months.

--oOo--

For instance, On December 9th, the Wardroom held its annual "Cocktail Party" at the Royal Hotel. The function was as great a success as ever, despite that the fifth year of war makes it necessary to imbibe homely beer in place of the many exclusive and exotic drinks of happier days. The spirit of camraderie, however, did not suffer, but was indeed enhanced in consequence.

--oOo--

One of my colleagues (who acts as 'newshawke' for "SpunYarn") tells me he spent a 'whale' of an evening at the Christmas Party for the Lower Deck, given in the Church Hall on December 27th, by Commander and Mrs. Bartley and the First Lieutenant. Everything went with a swing there was a Christmas tree with a present for everyone, some new games, which caused great merriment, the Dance Orchestra of the Maritime Regiment and refreshment in plenty. The proceedings however, had more than a touch of melancholy as Commander Bartley was leaving us, and Mrs. Bartley, who had been the motive power behind, not only this function, but other welfare work in the Base, was in bed with a chill, and could not attend. Both of them are sadly missed.

--oOo--

The New Year was only three days old when the Wren Officers at the Clifton Hotel threw another of their monumental parties. About 150 guests were present and greatly enjoyed the excellent stand - up supper, followed by dancing, when certain Senior Officers displayed unsuspected talent, and steps likely soon to be the rage in West - end ballrooms!

--oOo--

The usual Base Dances have been held at the Queen's Hotel, every fourth Monday, and have now reached a stage of popularity as to cause embarrassment to the organisers. For instance, it was with real regret that lack of space and pre-sale of tickets prevented our admitting a number of men, who were home on leave in January from overseas.

-26-

We have had the Winter Stage Show presented by the Ship's Club. This is described fully elsewhere in this issue, but suffice to say that it played to packed houses, and in my opinion the success of this new musical was well reflected in the enthusiasm of the audience.

--oOo--

On Tuesday February 29th, we bade farewell to Lieut. Commander J. Gurney Braithwaite, for so long our enthusiastic No.1. On the previous day, Lt.Cdr. Braithwaite had taken leave of his departmental staff at an informal little function. This was followed on the Tuesday by a gathering of Officers who wished to say aurevoir, after which the retiring 1st Lieutenant dropped in at the Ship's Club Smoking Concert for a final fare well to the Lower Deck.

--oOo--

SPORTS NOTES, continued from page 8.

H.M.S.WESTCLIFF 2nd XI. (Lost 6-5): By the narrowest of margins we almost broke the spell. Personally, I think we should have done, as success in a local derby is worth any "record". However this very keen contest was most enjoyable both for us and the boys farther up the road.

It is rumoured that we have played a few more games than the aforementioned, but why there is no official record or definite memory of them is inexplicable. Maybe at the time we unconsciously considered them not worthy of mention at any future date, or, perhaps, quite consciously considered them as not bearing mention at any date whatever. Suffice it to say, however, that lack of training and the "Floating" nature of our personnel have not prevented at least 11 men of H.M.S. Leigh from having an enjoyable "kick around" most Saturdays this season so far.

R.B.

With the Football Season almost over, our thoughts turn to Cricket. We have arranged for Pitches at Southchurch Park on alternate Saturdays and Wednesdays and all that now remains is to get some fixtures, and of course to get a side together. Last season we failed badly in the latter, and it is hoped that more will show interest in the summer game . If there are players among us now, please bring your gear back with you when next you go on leave. It is hoped to get some net-practice in before the season starts in May. Details will be announced in due course.

So far we have not had confirmation from the Thorpe Bay Tennis Club, that we may again use their Tennis Courts, but it is felt that this will be forthcoming in the near future, and a notice will be displayed.

-27-   H.S.N.

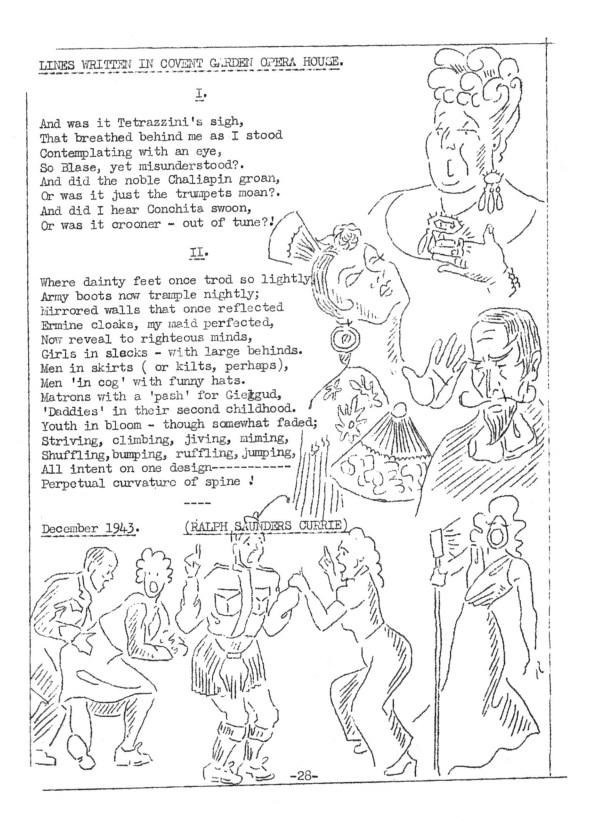

LINES WRITTEN IN COVENT GARDEN OPERA HOUSE.

I.

And was it Tetrazzini's sigh,
That breathed behind me as I stood
Contemplating with an eye,
So Blasé, yet misunderstood?.
And did the noble Chaliapin groan,
Or was it just the trumpets moan?.
And did I hear Conchita swoon,
Or was it crooner - out of tune?!

II.

Where dainty feet once trod so lightly,
Army boots now trample nightly;
Mirrored walls that once reflected
Ermine cloaks, my maid perfected,
Now reveal to righteous minds,
Girls in slacks - with large behinds.
Men in skirts (or kilts, perhaps),
Men 'in cog' with funny hats.
Matrons with a 'pash' for Gielgud,
'Daddies' in their second childhood.
Youth in bloom - though somewhat faded;
Striving, climbing, jiving, miming,
Shuffling, bumping, ruffling, jumping,
All intent on one design-----------
Perpetual curvature of spine !

————

December 1943.   (RALPH SAUNDERS CURRIE)

-28-

The following tribute to the Home Guard is extracted from the
Bulletin of the Fleet Street Branch of the British Legion.

The Home Guard is the unpaid, part-time, part worn, couponless
sockless, shirtless and breathless Army. Its Members are supposed to put
bullets in the bull of miniature targets (which they cannot see)   at 25
yards distance; to be ferocious bayonet fighters   (this entails making
extraordinary faces, grunting and grinding the teeth): to be also all-in
wrestlers and long distance runners. They are supposed to know the weight,
killing power, mechanism and working parts of the rifle, several machine
guns, countless grenades, and a number of strange sub-artillery weapons
to say nothing of truncheons, toggle-ropes, shot guns and pikes. When they
become proficient in any particular weapon it is immediately declared ob-
solete and a new one is substituted.   The idea of this is to ensure perpetual training and to prevent them digging for victory, going to the pictures or nursing the baby, in their spare time.   They are supposed to be
able to change themselves into nigger minstrels or Zulu medicine men, with
leaves in their hair, in a few seconds.   To make this sound easy this is
camouflage.   They have to know the location , front and back entrances of
all Wardens' Posts; Police Stations; Fire Stations; Dressing Stations;
Offices; Railway Stations; Police Call Boxes and Petrol Filling Stations.
They are supposed to be experts in fieldcraft, battlecraft, street-fight-
ing, all round defence - to know how to use natural cover and covering
fire, how to set a map, box a compass and splice the main-brace, how to
move unseen and unheard, (sometimes through the back entrance of the local)
how to crawl on a middle-aged tummy through under-growth, bricks and rub-
ble,   and how to convert themselves at the shortest notice from peaceful
citizens to bloody assassins.   They must know all about extermination,
decontamination, detonation, consolidation, abomination, to say nothing of
salvation.   They have to recognise and describe aeroplanes and tanks of
all nations at sight, and how to deal with them.   They must also support
the regulars which sometimes happens after closing time.   They frequently
mount 12 hours' guard, for which they are paid three bob, to spend on lux-
uries or lose at nap. They have to be able to deal with all known and unknown gasses; know how to balance forage caps on their heads when spring-
ing forward to the attack and how to provide themselves with iron rations
without any money, points or hope. Incidentally, they are supposed to earn
their own living, if time permits.

31.

- SPUN-YARN -

The Journal of the Thames Naval Control.

★ ★

PRICE SIXPENCE ★ SEPTEMBER ★ 1944

Page 3 with continuation page 30 is the 'Spunyarn Gazette'. These are the Honours and Awards pages with lots of Awards and Mentioned in Despatches for NCS members. It includes the award of a CBE to now Commodore J. P. Champion, DSO., RN. It also contains a very sad Obituary for Commander E. R. TAYOR, OBE., RD., RNR. Commander Taylor was killed by enemy action on 26th July 1944 having served with NCS since April 1941 and sailed 115 convoys.

Commander R. V. Rutley is no stranger to heroic exploits. It was he who 4 years before had organised the 'Retreat from Lorient'. Now in pages 4 - 8 entitled "D - PLUS 1" Commander Rutley recounts his exploits in charge of Operational Convoy One. This comprised large convoy vessels carrying "many thousands of tons of most important supplies for the invasion forces". His convoy left Southend on D - Day to arrive in France next day.

This well written story of his delivering Operational Convoy One ended officially when putting the convoy at anchorage off the French coast. Ever the adventurer, together with a journalist who had accompanied him from Southend, they stepped ashore to explore.

Of particular interest to me is Rutley's account on page 6, of his attempted visit to the village of Courseulles but being warned that the route was mined with work still required by engineers. My father, with the Royal Engineers attached to the 3rd Canadian Regiment, landed on Juno beach 6th June the day before Commander Rutley and by evening was holed up in an abandoned school in Courseulles. I recall my father, after the war, telling me that the Canadians he served with were the toughest most courageous men he had ever met. Most were very young agricultural or farm labourers. They were spirited and patriotic. My father was himself a very tough man. He had travelled the world for much of his working life as a merchant seaman (stoker) but was experienced, streetwise and self educated. He was old enough to be the father of the young Canadians. His assessment of them has stayed in my memory and of course is confirmed by the many accounts written of Canadians and the D-Day landings.

Page 9 "2000th CONVOY" has a short continuation but on the previous page 8. Commander in Chief, Admiral of the Fleet Sir John Tovey, GCB., KBE., DSO, accompanied by W. D. Stevens, Director of the Trade Divison attended a dinner at The Palace Hotel where congratulations to Capt. Champion as Guest of Honour were given. It was attended by many high ranking naval officers including Commodore R. G. H. Linzee CBE., DSO., Chief of Staff The Nore, Chatham.

Page 21 is a cartoon that needs no introduction.

HONOURS AND AWARDS.

"SPUN YARN" offers on behalf of its readers, the heartiest congratulations to the following Officers and Ratings of H.M.S. "LEIGH" who have received the undermentioned Awards, promulgated since our last issue: -

COMMANDER OF THE ORDER OF THE BRITISH EMPIRE: -

Commodore J. P. CHAMPION, D.S.O., R.N.

THE DISTINGUISHED SERVICE CROSS: -

Commander C. L. de H. BELL, R.D., R.N.R.
Commander F. A. G. HUNTER, R.D., R.N.R.
Commander H. E. MORISON, R.D., R.N.R.

THE DISTINGUISHED SERVICE MEDAL: -

Convoy Leading Signalman A. E. RUDKIN, LD/X.4212.

MENTIONED IN DESPATCHES: -

Commander A. AYRE, D.S.O., R.N.R.
Convoy Leading Signalman L. J. PARSONS, C/JX.269269.
Convoy Signalman J. F. MADDEN, C/JX.226576.
Convoy Signalman B. H. PRYOR, C/JX.233745.
-----oOo-----

OBITUARY.

It is with very deep regret that we record the death by enemy action, while on leave, of Commander E. R. TAYLOR, OBE, RD, RNR. Commander Taylor had been a Commodore of Convoy, attached to Southend,

(CONTINUED ON PAGE 30.)

- 3 -

"SPUN YARN GAZETTE" - Continued from PAGE 3.

from April 1941, until his death on 26th July, 1944. Commander Taylor sailed one hundred and fifteen convoys in this period, and earned during this time, the worthy regard of his colleagues, and the deep admiration and respect of the Signal Staffs who sailed with him. The death of Cdr. Taylor will come as a sad personal loss to all those who knew him well.

-----oOo-----

M A R R I A G E S:-

Wren J. WINCH-FURNESS and Mr. A. C. Boultwood......... 9th. April, 1944

Wren P. DENTON and Gunner P. Spiers....................18th. April, 1944

Wren A. COOPER and Trooper A. Williamson..............22nd. April, 1944

Wren M. J. HUNT and Tel. C. S. Allan.................. 5th. July, 1944

Wren D. ROBINSON and Ldg.Sto. F. Dye.................. 19th. July, 1944

Wren D. J. GRIMWADE and Mr. S. Freeman................ 22nd. July, 1944

Ldg.Wren E. WHITMILL and Cpl. J. Parker............... 7th. August 1944

P.O.Wren J. BLACKBURN and Lieut. F. L. HOGG, R.N.V.R..26th. August 1944

-----oOo-----

B I R T H:-

To LdgSig. E. WILLIAMS and Mrs.Williams- a son, Ian....18th. July 1944.

-oOo-----oOo-----oOo-----oOo-----oOo-----oOo-----oOo-----oOo-----oOo--

"SPUN YARN" - September, 1944.

ILLUSTRATIONS: Commander C. H. Williams, R.N.R.

PRINTED BY: Sigs. K.A.Sewell, W.G.Chaplin, J.T.Wood.

CIRCULATION: Sig. F. B. Goldsworthy.

EDITOR: Payr.Lieut. W. R. Milnes. R.N.V.R.

-:-:-:-:-:-:-:-:-:-:-

C.H.W.

By: Commander R. V. RUTLEY, O.B.E.,R.D.,R.N.R.

(When our armies evacuated France four years ago, the great River Thames played no small part in the feat of embarking and transporting the indomitable B.E.F. to safety. But this operation was an affair which was unpremeditated and improvised, though none the less glorious a one for all that. The Invasion of Normandy on the other hand was perhaps the most comprehensive scheme of deliberate military planning ever under taken by man. Once again Old Father Thames came right into the picture. Commander Rutley's narrative describes one aspect of what was merely the beginning of the outcome of many months of feverish planning and labour, the greater part of which cannot yet be told, and much of it never will be! The Thames Naval Control was once again enabled to render direct and spirited help in that vital function in which we claim to be the World's leading exponents - that of sailing ships! - N. B.)

--oOo--

It was on D. Day, 6th. June, 1944, that I left Southend, in command of Operational Convoy One. For weeks and months, English Ports had been doing the spade work of organising convoys of: Transport, Guns, Ammunition, and Supplies for the build-up of the Invasion Forces. Build-Up is only less vital than the initial assault, for without it the whole operation of the invasion of France would have been doomed to failure.

The Conference had been held at Southend under Commodore J. P. Champion, attended by the Senior Officer (Captain C. R. L. Parry) and other Commanding Officers of the Escort Vessels, together with the Masters of all the ships and transports comprising the Convoy. This convoy was a composite affair, details of which, even at this stage, cannot be divulged, but it contained among others, a number of large Merchant Vessels loaded with many thousands of tons of most important supplies bound for the Invasion Forces.

- 4 -

The weather was overcast and cloudy with a moderate wind in the west, but meteorological reports were generally favourable. So, with fair promise, the convoy weighed early in the morning, and proceeded for the Downs and the Straits of Dover. The Kentish coast was clearly visible on our starboard hand, and things went well until we were off Dover. The first opposition was experienced here from the enemy when his heavy guns opened fire from Cape Gris Nez, but only a few salvos were fired. The traffic in the Channel was really unbelievable, and we were continually meeting or overtaking all kinds of craft, so that from time to time, the navigation of the convoy was distinctly tricky.

Eventually, and dead on time, the first convoy of the Build Up arrived at the lowering position, and we were ordered to our position off the French coast, where we anchored. While steaming into our anchoring positions we passed Allied Battleships bombarding the coast, away to the East. This was replied to by German guns off Cape La Heve, and there were many fires ashore. Meanwhile gliders and transport planes were flying overhead, to land in a continuous stream behind the beaches. Adding to the uproar were the shells of our Cruisers, screaming over to drop on various targets two or three miles inland.

When the convoy anchored, my work as Commodore was finished pro. tem., so I decided to go ashore and see if I could assist the Naval Beachmaster in any way. I took with me the Marquis of Donegall, Merchant Navy Correspondent for the "Sunday Despatch" who had sailed with me from Southend. At this time four L.C.T's had arrived alongside to discharge mechanised vehicles and other equipment. On one of these we proceeded to the beach, accompanied by about ten vehicles of various descriptions. We landed on a sandy beach, with dunes which shelved very gradually towards the foreshore. Having grounded the L.C.T. and lowered the ramp, the No.1 took a sounding by boathook. He reported three-foot-six so the order was given to carry on discharging.

The first vehicle was a staff car, and into this jumped the driver and three officers. It was suggested that we did likewise, but from past experience of landing on open beaches by boat, I selected the second car, a Jeep. The passenger platform of this was a good deal higher than the staff car, and I wanted to see the first vehicle land safely before attempting it myself. The car was driven down the ramp, got about six yards, then struck a runnel and completely disappeared, turning over as it sank. The occupants fortunately escaped with a ducking! We hoisted the ramp and backed out to try and find a better beach. This time we grounded rather nearer the shore, but as luck would have it the ramp had jammed and an emergency repair tank was signalled. This came splashing alongside, but, good plumber's mate that he was, did not possess a small enough punch to knock out the pin and he was forced to go back and fetch one. Meanwhile the sergeant in charge gave us a ride ashore.

I jumped down on to French soil, quickly followed by Donegall. This was what I had been looking forward to since leaving France in

- 5 -

June, 1940. It was then I had been sent to Lorient, and had succeeded in getting all the British and Neutral shipping out of the port without any loss. We had been continuously "pasted" by the enemy, and had had no air cover. What a difference now, with a continuous stream of aircraft overhead. Fighters covering the landing, Troop-carriers and Gliders landing men, and in the Bay, Naval Forces ranging from Battleships to M.L's.

On landing, fifty yards to our right, was an ex-enemy block house where the Naval Beach Authorities were setting up their H. Q.   We

made our way towards this through masses of men, gear, tanks, guns, and vehicles of all sorts. A proper road there was not, but Engineers, working like demons, were improvising one above the high-water mark, along the various landing places.   On our way to the block-house, we passed several dead Germans and one Englishman. He was lying half-way up the escarpment to the block - house, with his right hand raised, and his left thrown backwards in the act of throwing a grenade into the block-house.   I muttered only two words to Donegall, but the prayer from my heart reached thousands, for we were certain that the man had not been ordered to carry out this gallant action, but had done it on his own initiative.

In the block-house we encountered a Naval Lieutenant who willingly showed us round. It was an eight-sided structure of cement, having an escarpment depth of probably seventy yards around from the seaward side, with a gradient of 1 in 3. He told us that it had been taken in the initial assault by a Sherman tank which had charged straight up and fired, making a direct hit on the heavy gun it housed. The jacket of the gun had been ripped off for a distance of some three feet and the shield battered and bent.

Having transacted my official business, and finding I could be of no more assistance on the beach, we decided to explore the village of Courseulles, lying about a mile and a half to the east.   Barbed wire entanglements were continuous to the rear of the sand dunes, intercepted at intervals by entrances to dug-outs and pill-boxes.   As we swung into the road, we met an Officer who warned us that the Engineers hadn't been over all the road, and mines might be encountered.   So we walked warily in the centre of the road, keeping a sharp look-out.   About two hundred yards along the road we encountered a corporal who conducted us around a fairly large dug-out.   Like the block-house, it was built of cement, and the walls appeared to be very thick. The roof consisted of steel girders with concrete above, again covered with a thick layer of earth and sand, so it would have been very hard to distinguish, even at a hundred yards. On a shelf at the back of this dug-out, lay a large electric torch.   My companion said it was a "peach of a torch" but we decided discretion was the better part of valour, as we had been warned of booby traps.   There

- 6 -

was also a small wireless set which appeared to be wired up to the usual aerial and earth. Again we did not twiddle the knobs to find out. By the amount of equipment discarded in this dug-out, it would appear that the Jerries had been in rather a hurry to leave.

We now proceeded towards the village, of which the shell only was left - the result of sea and air pounding. Before reaching it, we were stopped by an officer and picket who told us German snipers had been making their presence felt. Nevertheless we carried on for a mile and a half, and when within two hundred yards of the village, reached a small canal connecting the fishing basin with the sea. From here we could see, down the main street of the village, the havoc caused by the fighting. To reach the village itself would have meant a detour of four or five miles, and as dusk was falling we returned to the ship. On our way back we came across another German dug-out, and decided to have another look round. On the table was what appeared to be a case of maps, and having carefully investigated to see this was not connected in some way with wires or otherwise, I put it in my pocket. It was not until I arrived on board that I discovered the canvas case contained nothing of a more vital nature than an ersatz ground sheet!

Arriving back on the beach, we found that the next L.C.T. to leave for our ship had only two vehicles to discharge, so we went on board. It then transpired that the bull-dozer they had on board and were trying to discharge, would have to be turned round the right way before it could land. To add to the delay, the stern warp of the L.C.T. had fouled the warp of the L.C.T. in which we had landed. Now neither could move until the bull-dozer was got rid of. The time was now about 01.00, and Jerry decided to try and upset things by raiding the beach. A number of small anti-personnel bombs were dropped, one of which exploded on a petrol dump not thirty yards away. Not content with this, he also machine-gunned the landing craft. The First Lieutenant, Donegall, a Rating, and myself, all scrambled into the winch-house, and the rattle outside sounded like hail on a corrugated iron roof! Our L.C.T., of course, was returning the fire, while overhead still zoomed the shells of the Cruisers assisting our front-line. The tracer was cris-crossing all along the beach. It was not until 0200 that we managed to cut the kedge wire and transfer to the L.C.T. that had brought us ashore, leaving our friend to land the bull-dozer. On board again at 0230, the discharge of cargo was still proceeding. During the whole night there were air-raids punctuated by shells from German heavy guns to the east. About 0700 the next day we finished discharging, and with four other ships in the area steamed out to contact Captain Northbound Sailings from whom we received orders to sail next day. The night was enlivened by further E. Boat

- 7 -

and aircraft attacks.   Some time after midnight a ship to the eastward caught fire, either as a result of E. Boat attack or a shell from a gun ashore. She blazed for several hours, every part of her hull a glowing red.   At intervals there were explosions, and sparks could be seen in profusion. A terrible, yet wonderful sight, like a giant firework set-piece.

We sailed for England at 0950. We had with us several L.C. I's and L.C.T's, carrying prisoners and casualties, which were detached to their destinations while the main convoy proceeded without a further incident up-channel.   On approach to England the weather became foggy. The Merchant Navy Captains were looking forward to picking up pilots as we had all been up continuously from the beginning of the operation,but this was not to be.   We arrived at the rendezvous with no sign of the pilot cutter, so I decided to bring the convoy through. I received many signals, "When do we get a pilot?", but I had to reply, "Keep close and follow me".   In this way we managed to negotiate the remainder of our course in safety, and reached our destination. This was a fine piece of seamanship on the part of the Merchant Navy Captains, many of whom were unfamiliar with a difficult, and dangerous, passage - rendered all the more difficult by reason of the strain which for the previous week they and their crews had so manfully borne.

-----oOo--oOo--oOo--oOo--oOo--oOo--oOo--oOo--oOo--oOo--oOo--oOo--oOo-----

2,000TH CONVOY - Continued from PAGE 9.

welcomed the N.C.S. London contingent - Commander Guy, 2/O Rafarel, and 3/O. Stephenson - together with Lt.Col. The Hon. C. J. Lyttleton, M.R.A and Commanders Rutley and Ayre, Coastal Commodores.

The speeches which enlivened, and in some cases, decorated this very pleasant occasion, made clear how diverse are the ramifications of the work for which the Thames Naval Control is responsible, and reminded us how much we have been, and are, dependent upon the support, and co-operation of the Staffs so felicitously represented by our evening's guests. A hearty welcome was also extended to Capt.Neame, Surgeon Capt. Greeson, Paymaster Capt. Pearce, Commander Hindley-Smith, and Lt. Colonel Newling, R.M., - of H.M.S."Westcliff"- whose help during recent operations was suitably acknowledged by the Commodore.

As soon as the King had been honoured, the company settled down to a feast of sound advice and mutual congratulation from the many speakers called upon by Commander Marshall, the Mess President.   Space does not allow us to dilate upon these pearls of wisdom and oratory,but suffice it to say that when the gathering broke up, there was a general air of satisfaction, and it can be said that:- "A good time was had, by one and all!".

--oOo--oOo--oOo--oOo--oOo--

- 8 -

By:- Payr.Lieut.Cdr. N. BAIRD, R.N.

Little did we think on 7th May 1942, when we sailed the One
Thousandth Convoy from the Thames, that the day would dawn on twice that
number. That day was 21st July 1944, when the Two Thousandth Convoy (an
Operational Convoy to the Normandy Coast) weighed anchor, and sailed for
the Downs and the Straits of Dover.

It was fitting, therefore, that the Commander-in-Chief, Admiral of the Fleet Sir John Tovey, G.C.B.,K.B.E.,D.S.O., should visit us
together with Capt. J. D. Stevens, Director of Trade Division, in order
to address the Officers and Ship's Company. The Commander-in-Chief dwelt
upon the important part played in the build - up of the Normandy Beaches
and his expression of appreciation, for the support he had received from
Commodore Champion and his staff, was heard with no small pride by Naval
and W.R.N.S. Officers and Ship's Company. In the afternoon the Commander
in Chief inspected operations on the Pier, and addressed the Masters of
the 2,000th Convoy - then in conference. This convoy was to mark another
milestone in the war record of the River Thames.

Such an event as the sailing of 2,000 convoys - comprising
several scores of thousands of ships - could hardly be allowed to pass
uncelebrated. The Officers of the Base drank a sober cocktail - if that
is not a contradiction in terms! - after the conference, and the Ship's
Company Dance and Party is fully described elsewhere.

On the evening of sailing, the Officers of Thames Naval
Control brought the day's work to a fitting conclusion, at a dinner held
at the Palace Hotel,at which Commodore Champion was the guest of honour.
A goodly company of some seventy officers, including guests, attended.
Commodore R. G. H. Linzee. C.B.E.,D.S.C., Chief of Staff The Nore, was a
very welcome guest from Chatham Staff. Capt. Littleston, Cdr. Simmonds,
Payr.Lieut.Cdr's Millson and Fowler made a strong team from Trade Divis-
ion - the two latter being old members of the Southend Staff. We also
(CONTINUED ON PAGE 8.)

- 9 -

124

Route Orders

① Keep to the
   swept channel.

② Don't follow
   blindly in the
   wake of your
   next ahead.

– 21 –

Differences with Superiors and Pride in the Southend NCS Operation

John Champion was no stranger to battles with his superiors. He had pride in NCS operations in Southend and on one occasion had a 'tiff' with his seniors at Chatham. Monthly statistics on convoys out of East Coast ports e.g. Lowestoft, Yarmouth etc. mentioned only the number of convoys that each had sailed. However, the number of ships in a convoy was not mentioned. The numbers leaving Southend were far greater than anywhere else with difficult navigation of the Nore sandbank in cooperation with Admirals C in C the Nore. Up to 60 ships may have sailed in a convoy from Southend and even taking an average throughout the war the number was 25. Many leaving Southend were then 'buttoned' by others to take advantage of the battleship escorts and air cover. At the beginning there was no air cover and many more convoy ships were sunk by enemy aircraft than later in the conflict. Captain Champion complained that the convoy statistics should reflect the more difficult task that Southend had in managing the largest number of vessels in its convoys. He was reprimanded in a letter suggesting he was making a storm in a teacup. Although diplomatic in response, Champion left his detractors in no doubt as to his views on the matter. On 30th April, 1942 an FN convoy comprised 113 ships.

Keeping ships in their convoy assembled positions was not easy especially when sailing in the dark and trying to stay in the narrow mine swept lanes. The slow speed of a convoy made it vulnerable to attack from the air and by the very fast 'schnellboot' (E-boat). Therefore the battleship escorts were essential and accounted for many hits on German dive bomber aircraft, E-boats and submarines but not without coming under fierce attack themselves. There were a number of regular destroyer escorts throughout the war including HMS Wallace and HMS Westminster. HMS Wallace was known as "One round Wallace" because it had a habit of shooting down enemy aircraft with its first round. On 26th January 1941 HMS Wallace with HM Drifters Fisher Boy and Reids, successfully engaged enemy aircraft which attacked shipping off the East Coast, shooting down a Junkers 88 and an Me 110.

Aboard HMS Wallace, which made at least 100 escort trips along the East Coast's 'bomb alley', as it was known, was one Sub Lt. HRH Prince Philip. Prince Philip joined HMS Wallace in January 1942 and within nine months was promoted First Lieutenant. By all accounts a most intelligent and accomplished naval officer, Prince Philip's duties were carried out in the least glamourous of naval war arenas. In making trips from Methil or Rosyth in Scotland to Southend I would like to think that he was familiar with Southend Pier.

Destroyer Escort HMS Wallace

Prince Philip as a young naval officer who joined HMS Wallace on convoy duties in 1942

There is a story quoted that in HMS Wallace as the lead destroyer Prince Philip observed that on HMS Westminster as second lead, were some "funny looking balls hoisted at the back of the bridge". He received news that these were a type 994 radar aerial. The story then goes on to say that Prince Philip wished to know why, as Flotilla Leader they did not have these on HMS Wallace. In truth the three balls hanging behind the bridge on HMS Westminster were a souvenir trophy taken from outside a pawnbroker's shop in Newcastle.

There was another occasion when Prince Philip saved HMS Wallace and its crew from almost certain sinking by bomber aircraft. During July to August 1943 she escorted convoys en-route to the invasion of Sicily (Operation Husky). A German bomber had spotted HMS Wallace and attacked her in darkness several times, returning every 20 minutes to make a hit. It would be only a matter of time before it succeeded. The quick thinking of Prince Philip gave him the idea of setting fire to a carley raft and releasing it aft of the ship where it would be billowing with smoke and fire as a decoy. The intention was to make the German bomber believe it had scored a hit last time round. It worked because the plane returned and attacked the raft believing it was finishing the job. Meanwhile HMS Wallace sped off in the darkness; cut its engines and waited until the all clear.

HMS Westcliff

On 20th May 1942 secret instructions were received from Commander in Chief the Nore for the requisitioning of suitable property in Southend with a view to the formation of a Combined Operations Base. The instructions envisaged requiring accommodation for 600 officers and 5,000 men. The police enabled NCS to trace the absentee owners of properties that were to be requisitioned mainly at Westcliff, just above the seafront. Combined Operations Holding and Training Base to be known as HMS Westcliff was established. Much of the administration of this new command structure was to be undertaken by WRENS. Some re-allocation of accommodation already occupied had to be made as there were to be 600 WRENS as

well as 40 nurses and 50 Voluntary Aid Detachment workers. HMS Westcliff was to become an important training and nursing facility.

In another of his Germany Calling broadcasts Lord Haw Haw announced, to great amusement in Southend, the sinking of two British ships; HMS Leigh and HMS Westcliff!!

HMS St. Matthew

At Burnham on Crouch a further base was established as a key defence establishment with links to the River Roach, Foulness Island, Wallasea Island and river routes off the Thames.

All of these shore bases were part of the NCS and Captain Champion's responsibilities.

A.P. Herbert (AP)

A. P. Herbert RNVR was a WWI navy veteran. From the comfort of retirement in Teddington 'messing about on the river' in his boat Water Gypsy, AP found himself in his 50's recruited for WWII special duties patrolling the River Thames from Teddington to Southend.

A. P. Herbert was best known as a novelist, playwright, lyricist for pre-war West End musicals and a regular contributor to 'Punch' magazine. He was also an independent MP, a law maker and a friend of Winston Churchill. Winston called him 'The funniest man in England and perhaps the wisest'. A P Herbert, who died 50 years ago, employed the English language as if he had invented it all by himself. Comedy was never more succinct:

> *Holy Mother, we do believe*
> *That without sin thou didst conceive*
> *May we now in thee believing*
> *Also sin without conceiving.*

In his post war writings and his autobiography there is a lot written about the years spent patrolling the river from Teddington to Southend. AP's boat Water Gypsy was requisitioned by the navy, painted battleship grey and mounted with a Lewis gun. Fortunately for him, AP was allowed to continue operating his boat as a Petty Officer with a small crew. Although AP's destination down the Thames was to a spot just off Canvey Island a lot of his time was spent visiting the HQ, Naval Control Service, Southend.

In his autobiography A. P. Herbert stated that his favourite place along The Thames was Canvey Island and in particular the Lobster Smack pub. The pub and its grounds stand many feet below sea level surrounded above by a sea wall built in the early 1600's by the Dutch and it was about this time the Lobster Smack was built. Early bare fist battles were fought as contests between the captains of ships. In the early days the captain aboard a ship might be the toughest and most brutal of the crew. In the 1850's there were many bare knuckle prize fights in the yard of the pub. In 1857 the great Tom Sayers fought Aaron Jones and the fight lasted 3 hours and 65 rounds. When it got dark and they could not see the bout was called a draw!

AP was a good pianist and wrote of an evening when he played piano in the pub surrounded by soldiers. It was getting late and Mr. Went the publican approached him. "Mr. Herbert" said Went. "You must stop playing otherwise I will get into trouble with the law." "I am the law" said AP and carried on playing.

On Sundays AP would play hymns on the piano for American soldiers and airman who stood in the yard outside for Sunday services. There were many American servicemen stationed here.

The Lobster Smack today and beloved of A. P. Herbert in wartime, near where his boat was permanently moored.

American B17 air crash at Canvey Point

A large number of B17 Flying Fortress bombers were returning to their base at Kimbolton from a bombing raid on the German V rocket launching site at Zudausques nr. Calais. One of the B17's, damaged in the raid, suddenly dropped down onto a B17 below, killing the pilot and co-pilot and slicing off one wing. The plane below crashed while the one above went down at All Hallows near Rochester. Some crew members bailed out in time but others were killed. Older members on Canvey Island remember this tragedy very well. Below is a mural on the sea wall at Canvey commemorating the dead American airmen.

Pilot - Lloyd L. Burns
Bombadier - Jack Gray
Co-Pilot - Fred Kauffman
Navigator - Edward N. Sadler
Tail Gunner - Louis W. Schulte
Radio Op./ Gunner - Leroy J. Monk
Waist Gunner - Richard Andrews
Ball Turret Gunner - William H. Farmer
Top Turret Gunner - Leonard F. Gibbs
Waist Gunner - Richard L. Billings

CREATED BY OPEN ARTS PLUS GUEST ARTIST

Normandy D-Day preparations at Southend including U.S. Navy's 32 Ships anchored off the Pier

Preparations - U.S. Navy loaded with U.S. Canadian and British Army Troops at the Pier. Nevile Shute - His Journey into Normandy from Southend with the U.S. Navy

Notes extracted from Commodore Champion's 1945 end of term log (not released to the public until 1972 under orders from The War Office)

The most intensive organisation and preparations of the war took place in Southend in the lead up to D-Day. The number of officers on the Pier was increased to 38 including 19 British, 17 Norwegian, one Dutch and one Belgian Officer.

Due to the secrecy necessary a force of U.S. Navy craft carrying tanks and filled with army troops arrived in Southend two and a half months later than originally planned. A Combined Forces Operation known as Force Group L.3 of the U.S. Navy arrived in Southend on 12th May 1944. The force comprised 32 LST's (Landing Ships Tank) under the command of U.S. Navy captain J. D. Shaw. This left only 3 weeks for organisation and training in what everyone understood to be the greatest invasion in the history of warfare - to an, as yet, unrevealed destination.

A house in Royal Terrace was requisitioned as the HQ for the captain of Force Group L.3. The Pier Hotel (close to The Palace Hotel) was also requisitioned as an Officers' Mess. An old searchlight station at the pier head was equipped as a signal station for exclusive use of the American force.

Facilities were given for Force Group L.3 to practice landing exercises in Thorpe Bay and elsewhere. There was great cooperation between the force and Captain Champion's team. The work of preparation for D-Day was only made possible by the wholehearted realisation by all officers, ratings and civilians of both sexes. Captain Champion made clear the historical importance of the operation.

LST 157 on which Nevile Shute travelled to Normandy with Captain J. D. Shaw. At Southend each of Force Group L.3's LST's were fitted with two kite balloons by pier staff.

The size of D-Day preparations was out of all proportion to anything hitherto experienced in five years of NCS operations at Southend. Additional harbour craft had to be secured. XDO Sheerness loaned 10 drifters. These were invaluable together with 10 LCV (P)'s. (Landing Craft Personnel).

On Monday 5th June five conferences were held at the Pier Head - 0900 - 1100 -1400 - 1800 and 2000 hrs. The secret destination known to Captain Champion was now revealed to the ships' officers at the conference briefings.

On departing for France, Captain Shaw expressed himself entirely satisfied with the support received at Southend.

Nevile Shute RNVR

Commodore Champion's 1945 log detailed the events surrounding U.S. Navy Captain J. D. Shaw at Southend but does not mention Nevile Shute.

Why was Nevile Shute assigned to accompany Captain J. D. Shaw with Force Group L3 for the Overlord D-Day Landings?

Under his full name of Nevile Shute Norway this multi-talented man ran his own very successful aeronautical business following employment as an aeronautical engineer with the Vickers Company. Shute used his full name to separate these activities from his already blossoming fame as a novelist where he was known simply as Nevile Shute. In his aircraft business in the 1930's he invented a multi engined training plane known as the Airspeed Oxford. It was used by the RAF and a total of 8,500 were manufactured. As a part time yachtsman he decided to join the Royal Naval Volunteer Reserve as a sub-lieutenant. By the end of the war he was a Lieutenant Commander.

Nevile Shute's celebrity as a writer drew the attention of the Ministry of Information for recruitment as a war correspondent. Apart from his D-Day assignment he went on to record in other war arenas, including Burma.

Shute's four part record of his D-Day experience with U.S. Captain Shaw is titled "Journey into Normandy" and the full account is lodged with his Foundation papers in Cambridge. If you wish to access this it is available online under 'Nevile Shute Journey into Normandy'. As it is very long I have summarised as best I can using his actual words without missing out important facts but in doing so have very occasionally needed to paraphrase.

Journey into Normandy
by Nevile Shute

Part 1

"My journey to Courseulles began at the royal Aircraft Establishment in Farnborough in England, curiously for a naval officer. My job is to produce experimental weapons for the changing needs of war; I have sat for four years in an office in the Admiralty with occasional trips to sea to see my things go wrong. Because I have been tired and weary with this work, from time to time I have amused myself by writing fictional romances in my bedroom in he evenings, and these stories have pleased others besides me. In the spring of 1944 I found myself carrying on two jobs at the same time, producing weapons for the war in the Far East and writing articles about the war in the Near West.

I was at Farnborough on Thursday June 1st when a telephone call came from the Admiralty to report next morning with all equipment and two blankets. I got to London that night and slept at my club and at 09.15 next morning I was in the Admiralty for a briefing with other correspondents. I have never been very clear about my own position. I went to Courseulles as a naval officer with no duty but to write what and when I chose, and with no responsibilities. Looking back upon it now, it was the perfect assignment.

We were not told very much that was of interest to the enemy but that the percentage of numbers if ships in the operation would be 60% British and 40% U.S. Of larger ships 75% would be British. We were told that there would be 4,000 ships in the operation of a size to get there under their own power. In conclusion we were told a saying of a British Admiral, Admiral Creasy, which I think deserves to go on record. "What Phillip of Spain failed to do, what Napoleon tried and failed to do, what Hitler never had the courage to do, we are about to do".

We were told our allocations. Most of the party were to go in motor coaches to the Solent district to embark in various craft. I was detailed to go to Southend, at the mouth of the Thames, to be embarked in Force L, the follow up to Force J. I was disappointed in this since I had applied for permission to go with them for the assault in an LCT carrying Priests. Instead of that I was to sail in an LST of the follow up force. One war correspondent was allocated to the follow-up force with me, Mr. John Marshall of the London Evening News. He was put in my charge. It was impossible to let Mr. Marshall travel in a public train after briefing, so I got an Admiralty car for him and we went down in comfort to Southend, that warm sunny morning.

At Southend we reported to the office of the Commodore in Charge and were passed to the office of the U.S. Navy next door. From there we were sent to a hotel requisitioned as accommodation for naval officers. We were told we would have to stay there several days before embarking. That afternoon, Captain J. D. Shaw of the U.S. Navy came over to see us to check our identity and give us our orders. I mention that courtesy because it struck me at the time that a Post Captain on the busiest day of his career might well have sent for a war correspondent and a lieutenant commander to wait upon him in his office. I was allocated to his flagship and Marshall to another ship. Captain Shaw commanded a force of 32 Tank Landing Ships, big diesel engine vessels of about 4,500 tons.

We embarked next day at 1700 hrs. taking all our gear down to the pier with the assistance of a couple of ratings and embarked in an LCVP (Landing Ship Vehicle Personnel). Each LST carried two LCVP's in davits. The flagship was loaded to capacity. She had three Sherman tanks on the tank deck, equipped for clearing land mines, and a number of small scout cars. In all, upon her tank deck she carried seventy three vehicles and about two hundred and fifty men in addition to thirty RAMC personnel. In this ship however, with Captain Shaw and his staff we had thirty six officers where normally there would be only nine. We caused the ship's officers much inconvenience. Instead of complaining as they might well have done they could not do enough for us. They gave us little presents in their anxiety to help which I found rather touching. One of them gave me a little Gideon Bible inscribed "From the boys of the US Navy vessel LST.... Which will stay with me for the rest of my life.

After learning our destination I observed the officers sitting together studying their maps. A time comes when you know the map absolutely without needing to look at it as though you had been there before. The beach they were studying was opposite the little town of Courseulles-sur-Mer. I leaned over their shoulders to study with them. Juno sector, beaches Mike and Nan. Juno meant that Force J was attacking there. These beaches were subdivided, as is usual into red, white and green according to the lights of a ship when heading in to the beach. I learned to my surprise on Saturday that D-Day was on Monday, and that we were to sail next morning at 0915 hrs. I had not thought it would be so soon. That night I slept in comfort by the kindness of Captain Shaw, on a settee in his day cabin made up as a berth.

At six thirty next morning I was up and doing, because there were religious services on board that I wanted to attend. Catholics in the tank deck and Protestants forward on the upper deck where we stood grouped between Bofors and Oerlikon guns in the cold windy morning light. We then learned that our departure had been delayed for 24 hours. When eventually we were ready to depart the weather outside was glorious. It took courage to believe that a gale was predicted. All Sunday morning the wind rose. The sky darkened , the sea rose; it rained a little. At 10 O'clock on Sunday night it was blowing a Force 7 in the Western English Channel and Force 5 in the Eastern part. It was considered that no landing craft could cross the channel in anything worse than Force 4. In the days that followed it was learned from German radio that nobody but crazy lunatics like Eisenhower and Ramsay would risk their men by starting an operation in such weather. It showed, they said, how pathetically and grossly incompetent was the Anglo-American command. In fact the Germans had withdrawn their entire E-boat and U-boat fleet to port on Sunday thinking that no operation could begin in such unsettled weather.

No German aircraft came to spy on us that we knew of. We passed through Dover without being shelled, we saw no E-boats and no U-boats. We passed unscathed from London River to Courseulles in thirty six hours as if there was no war at all, save that we lost one LST that strayed from the swept channel into a minefield. The Germans were taken completely by surprise.

Part II

German air reconnaissance seems to have been so cautious as to be practically useless to them. Our own experience has been that to be effective air reconnaissance must be bold. You can learn a little of your enemy by taking vertical photographs of his harbours from thirty thousand feet on the occasional cloudless day but it is very little. If you really want to find out what he is doing you must take a Spitfire or a Lightning and plaster it with automatic cameras, and pick a fearless young pilot and brief him to fly at zero feet immediately beside what you want to see, with all his cameras whizzing at top speed. The Germans never did that to us. We did it to them. We wanted to find out whether they had mines attached to their underwater obstacles upon the beaches so we put cameras into the nose of a Lightning and flew it up and down the beaches of France at low tide at about ten feet altitude. I do not know how many pilots lost their lives upon this duty, but their photographs were invaluable in showing the condition of the beach obstacles. Those British and American pilots who secured this information deserve more than a passing thought. About three in the morning of Tuesday 6th June, D-Day a squadron of two heavy four engine aircraft passed above us, towing Horsa gliders on their way to France. We wished them luck.

We sailed all day with little incident save that our steering failed on two occasions swinging us round at right angles to our course. The steering on an LST is electrical and relays sometimes get tired and fall out of clutch. We encountered what turned out to be an LCT Mark V floating upside down in the water. That evening we were anchored off Courseulles, the crew of two officers and nine men from this LCT were brought on board us because they were Americans of the U.S. navy and we were an American flagship. We came to the coast of Normandy about 1600 hrs. on the afternoon of D-Day and we anchored off the little town of Courseulles about 1700 hrs. The beach was littered with wrecked landing craft and shot up vehicles. The tide, which at this place had a rise and fall of about 23 feet was ebbing disclosing a long stretch of sand. The beach here has a gradient of about 1 - 100. Beyond the beach were sand hills beyond which were a few scattered houses and farms. The houses were much shot up. The craft upon the beach did not look too bad from where we were. Some had obviously been shelled but many of them seemed merely to have been beached and left by the receding tide as if they would get off the next tide.

We anchored about two miles from the shore. The anchorage was already crowded with other LST's and coasters and a few warships. The sea was now rough again for boat work. When we anchored the Rhino Ferries were still unloading LST's that had arrived before us. About 1800 hrs. all unloading stopped in Juno sector. The troops from the first wave were on shore and fighting well inland. We were now unable to land any more vehicles or stores or reinforcements to support the men on shore. As soon as this position became apparent it was terribly distressing. The success of the whole operation depended we felt on landing the reinforcements we had brought. Captain Shaw had a boat lowered and went off to the flagship of the sector, HMS Hilary accompanied by his liaison officer to ask if he might put his ships upon the beach to unload. He got a rather chilly reception from a very junior officer who told him that he must go back to his flotilla and wait for orders.

I was concerned when Captain Shaw came back. I had been for exercises in Hilary and I knew a number of her staff officers fairly well. I knew them to be both courteous and competent and not in the least likely to behave discourteously to an American Post Captain however busy they may be. I had a tenuous duty to report myself in Hilary as a naval officer functioning on his own as a writer within the diocese. I offered to go to Hilary for this purpose if Captain Shaw wished and to present his case to my friends in the right quarters on the flagship. It was decided that we should leave it until the morning. If no orders came by then I should go and try my hand as an ambassador.

It was dusk and from our anchorage we could see a long stretch of coastline to the eastwards. Bernieres was the next town down the coast from Courseulles, two or three miles on and that town seemed to be continuous with St. Aubin further on again. There were fires in these towns. The warships in the anchorage behind us were bombarding the coast in support of the troops on shore. We could see shell bursts on the beaches and in the town. It seemed to us that the Germans were getting out and setting fire to important buildings before they went. They had been there four years and no doubt they had whole buildings full of papers and files that they could not remove and had to burn. Alternatively it may have been wanton destruction to prevent us from having use of the buildings.

So passed the night of D-Day and now this seems a proper moment to digress and tell a story of the assault which I did not see. I travelled back on the night of D + 2 with a Brigadier who had gone in with the assaulting tanks in the vicinity of St. Aubin. I must not tell his name because on D-Day he ought to have been sitting at his desk in England. He was hurrying back now to England after a breath of the fresh air of war to try to slip back into his office chair and look as if he had only just been out for a cup of coffee. (The Brigadier gave a detailed account to Shute of the landings and the battle he witnessed).

Part III

One little anecdote told by the Brigadier. They had all been very seasick on the way over. The LCT (A) grounded and dropped its ramp. The first tank drove down into the shallow water as the German guns opened fire on them. Inside the tank the driver turned his head to the Brigadier as they roared up the beach. "Thank God we're off that bloody ship sir", he said. "I know what to do now". So they went into action.

No instructions reached us during the night. By morning Captain Shaw had thirty-one loaded LST's of his flotilla anchored and awaiting orders to unload. The sea was quite rough and the wind strong. At seven o'clock I went off in an LCVP to the flagship HMS Hilary to see what I could glean for Captain Shaw about the prospect of unloading. One of HMS Hilary's accommodation ladders had been smashed to matchwood by boats in the rough sea and the other did not look inviting with the rise and fall of the water. We edged up to the side and I made a jump for a rope ladder and went on board while my boat laid off to wait for me.

In the Operations Room I found Commander Edwards, Staff Officer (Plans) who had looked after me on the operational exercises. In less than five minutes he gave me the complete picture. I said that Captain Shaw had been waiting with his loaded LST's for twelve hours with no instructions to unload. I said that he wanted to get on with the war as we all did. Commander Edwards said that he was on no account to beach his ships without orders. There were other ships to unload before those of Captain Shaw's flotilla and to put stuff on the beach in the wrong order would not be helpful. For the moment he said the Army on shore were all right. Captain Shaw would get his instructions on when and where to beach. I was very impressed and left Hilary after less than five minutes feeling that everything was in control and being handled by people who knew exactly what they were doing. I hope I succeeded in conveying this impression to Captain Shaw and I had a crack at it in the wardroom over breakfast.

A few bombs fell on the beach that morning, D+1 dropped by German fighters that dived through the cloud, dropped their bombs at random on the crowded beach and vanished back into the cloud.

(It was such an action that on one day my father who landed with the Third Canadian Regiment at Courseulles on D-Day was blasted by a bomb dropped by a German plane and injured but not killed. As a Royal Engineer in Inland Water Transport he had been given a large rucksack battery-pack attached to a metal detector. His job was to clear beach mines to allow troops to come ashore more safely. After a short while on a hospital ship he was looked after by nuns before being sent for recuperation at Netley in Hampshire. He discharged himself to return to his unit a.s.a.p. The bomb had blasted sand into his legs. Years after the war I remember he would sit picking grit out of his legs with a penknife as it came to the surface. About once a year he could peel the skin from his arms like a long pair of gloves due to a skin condition. He made light of it all because he survived when many including close friends around him did not).

At about 1300 hrs. an LCVP was going on some errand from the flagship. I asked Captain Shaw if this boat might put me on the beach. It was not very easy to decide how to land upon the beach when we got near. Many of the beach obstacles were still in place and sticking up out of the water. I did not want to risk the boat and her crew by taking them through these particularly as I did not know that they had not still got mines tied to them. Finally I selected a wrecked LCT Mark III that lay upon the beach. The ebbing tide would soon leave her dry. We edged the boat up to her stern and I got on board her and our boat backed away to safety.

The tide went down and presently I walked delicately ashore from the wrecked LCT treading carefully in the wheel tracks until I could find more about the situation in regard to mines. I reached the roadway and went west along the beach till I came to the Beachmaster's party, meaning to report myself. I know him slightly, Lt. Cdr. Lowndes and I

knew his army colleague Colonel Humphries. They greeted me cheerfully and gave me and old German slit trench to sleep in. The Germans they said had had to get out so hurriedly that they had been unable to take down their own notices of the minefields and in many places the word MINEN showed the danger spots.

I had brought with me to the beach all that I could carry readily. Gas mask, tin hat and duffle coat, revolver and ammunition plus two twenty four hour ration packs, camera and writing materials. All these made quite a load and I was glad to dump most of it in the slit trench. I started off along the beach to walk towards Courseulles. Presently I came to the first German pillbox, a large concrete structure jutting out from the sandhills to enfilade the beach. It contained a field gun on wheels, an old gun once drawn by horses with wooden wheels and iron tyres. In front of the pillbox on the sandy beach lay two or three dead Canadian soldiers as they had fallen. Many had been removed inland but in about two miles of beach I saw around 15 dead Canadians and one dead German.

I left the beach and passed through the sandhills and along a track towards the little hamlet of Graye-sur-Mer. The river Seulles runs into the sea at this point. The track by which I went passed by a patch of rough ground and scrub, perhaps three hundred yards in diameter. Opposite this patch I met a soldier walking casually in the opposite direction. He said "I wouldn't hang about here sir. There's a sniper in there, comes up and pots at someone now and then" and he pointed to a line of British soldiers, tense and alert with Sten guns and rifles at the ready going slowly through the patch like beaters. I wish very much I had been wearing khaki and not blue and walked on to Graye. Later that afternoon I heard that they had caught this sniper. He was a lad of sixteen and he thought that he was to be shot immediately. The Germans had told their men that the English shot all prisoners they took and the boy believed it.

I heard next day that two German women had been found behind a hedge with a trench mortar, lobbing bombs onto the beach now and then. I did not see these women myself but I believe it to be true. My own guess is that they were German prostitutes with the army who had taken up weapons at the invasion. The Geman army in this sector was composed very largely of foreigners. Thirty per cent of the prisoners we took were Poles and at the time I landed there were fifty Russians still holding out in a wood up on a hill within sight of the beach giving not much trouble and clearly not knowing what they had better do. We cleaned them up next day and took them all prisoner. When I grew hungry and tired I began to trace my steps towards the beach and my slit trench, picking up my blanket and mineral water on the way. It was a fine evening and the ships were beginning to beach upon the sand. Unloading was still proceeding at top speed from LCT's and LCI's still coming from England. I dug out my slit trench a bit and sat down for a supper of mineral water and twenty four hour ration. Presently it seemed to me that another blanket would not go amiss, and so I set out to walk west along the beach.

German prisoners were coming down to the beach in a long file and embarking in an LCT under a heavy guard. They looked no different to any prisoners I had seen in illustrated papers. They were not defiant. They looked rather a poor lot but I fancy that all prisoners look like that because they are prisoners. Some of them looked very young indeed and the men by me were all commenting on it. We thought that some of them could not have been more than fourteen years old.

I came to a sad place where a jeep had towed a six pounder anti-tank gun up to high water mark. A shell from one of the shore batteries had hit the gun and shattered it in to several pieces and machine guns had riddled the jeep through so that it would never run again. The men who manned it had long left or else had been removed but their equipment was there and scattered over the loose sand in utter confusion. I took a clean new blanket for my bed and walked back rather sadly to my trench and made my bed. War is a harsh business.

After spending a bad night I walked into Courseulles after breakfast to inspect the town. I had only seen the front the previous day. As I walked up one main street old men stopped me every hundred yards to shake me by the hand and tell me how glad they were that we had come. The town itself was in a condition of light blitz. That is to say there were a few houses demolished and much window glass had been removed but the water was still running and the electricity still worked. I went into the Church. A shell had burst upon he roof at the west end so that one corner of the nave was open to the sky, but within the church everything was quiet and tidy and peaceful, ready for a service. I left the church and walked up the street. The one street was thronged with army traffic heading northwards from the beaches. The street narrow, with sharp corners, and the congestion was bad. DUKW's in particular were having difficulty because of their great length and at one corner they had to reverse to get round causing much delay to the traffic stream. The military police were on the job and controlling the traffic very efficiently, making the best of a difficult job.

In this traffic stream were vehicles that had crossed with me in LST 517, so she had unloaded in the end. One Canadian officer that I had met upon the ship asked me the situation inland. I got upon the step of his half track truck and rode with him a little way while I showed him on his map the situation as I knew it. Then I wished them luck and got off and walked back to find a place where I could sit and write. I settled in an estaminet (small café) and sat there writing and talking to whoever came in for two or three hours. They had quite good light wine both white and red and they had cognac but no other drinks. No beer and none of the drinks such as Pernod that they would have sold in quantities in former days. The men and women that passed through the estaminet that morning did not look underfed. They looked well and healthy just as French country people always had looked. I was surprised by the number of young men in evidence, men of about thirty or thirty five years of age. The boy who served me in the estaminet showed me his call up papers to go and work in Germany. We came just in time for him.

I finished my writing and took it down to the Beach Headquarters in the early afternoon for despatch to the Admiralty via Hilary. My time upon the beach was drawing to a close. I had seen most of what I had come to see and I was growing very tired. I prowled around all afternoon gleaning such information as remained. I talked to a young officer with three mine clearing tanks. Two of his three tanks were out of action for repair, for though they detonate the mines they suffer frequent damage in the process. The beach was thronged that afternoon with beached ships of all sizes up to about four thousand tons, a most extraordinary sight. I took a lot of photographs and made my way back to my gear in the slit trench. Right opposite me high and dry was upon the beach was LST 535 another of those hospitable American ships. I went on board her at about 1900 hrs. and asked her young captain Lt. Olsen U.S.N.R. for a passage home.

That night the tide came up. The Captain filled his ballast tanks and held the vessel down upon the sand till he had more than his light draught of water,

then pumped his tanks out and came up and floated. We slid off and out to sea but I knew nothing about that. I was asleep. D-Day + 2 and we were on our way home.

U.S. Navy Captain J. D. Shaw. Operational Record 3rd November 1950

At the outbreak of the Korean War U.S. Navy Captain J. D. Shaw was Commander of United States Naval Station, Tongue Point, Astoria, Oregon. The Captain mustered the ship's crew of LST (Landing Ships Tank) 762 for the re-commissioning of the ship for the Korean War. The crew were marched to ship NH 83851 USS APL 49 where commissioning of LST 762 took place pursuant to US Navy regulations.

Revenge and justice for two five year old children

It is November 1944. In July, Southend NCS 2,000th convoy was sailed. Troops had invaded Normandy and were advancing through France. John Champion had just received his CBE and at the Southend Base Ships Club members were dancing to the records of Victor Sylvester. In Stadium Road two five year olds at play after their tea were about to go hand in hand to visit their school on a mission. They became locked in the school until night time and were eventually rescued by the police, an ARP warden and the school's caretaker.

Me and my cousin Jean Peirson had joined Bournemouth Park Road infants school in March of 1944 both just 5 years old, Jean being six days younger than me. Since Jean arrived with her mother from Wales the two of us became inseparable. After school we would have our tea and play in the street.

Jean was living at No. 17 Stadium Road with her mother and my maternal grandmother, the mother of Jean's father serving in Germany. I lived at the other end of the street at No. 4.

On 30th November 1944 and meeting up as usual after our tea, we got to discussing how we felt discriminated against by our teacher during our six months in her class. Miss Essex had her favourites and that certainly did not include Jean and me. Behind Miss Essex' high chair overlooking the class, was a large double door cupboard. This cupboard contained black tin paint boxes, paint brushes and jam jars. There were Players 50's cigarette tins containing plasticine and there were toys. Did we ever get handed a toy? Never. I wanted the box containing cut out tin fish, with fishing rod and magnet for picking up the fish. Jean and I only ever got the tins of paints (one between us where others had one each) or the 50 Players cigarette tin with rock hard plasticine that by the end of a lesson was just about soft enough to roll into a ball. There was an old butler sink over by the window for filling the jam jars for painting. I always smoothed my brush across the jam jar to squeeze off excess water. Jean put a water filled brush into the paints and flooded them. I would lose interest in painting and lean forward to pull the plait of Dawn Smith who sat in front of me. I got told off. It was all Jean's fault.

Having decided to do something about this 'discrimination' we went hand in hand and walked the quarter mile to the school. We entered unseen and went to our classroom. Out came the paints. We spread out lots of paintings on the floor. I took the much coveted box with fishing rod and tin fish from the cupboard. I was bored with it in minutes.

We heard the caretaker in the hall and hid behind our desks. He did not see us and went on to lock up the school. We continued and had a great time. Discrimination it seemed was not confined to the classroom. In the hall behind a curtain were musical instruments. There were tambourines, triangles and drums. I wanted a drum but always ended up with a triangle. So, out came a drum. Meanwhile Jean mounted the stool of the school piano and while she plonked away on the keys I beat the drum.

It was already dark and we decided it was time to go. The doors were locked. I took off one of my wellington boots and threw it at the glass window of the door. Glass in doors was reinforced with anti-blast wire. The welly bounced off. Jean started crying. I remember saying "Don't cry or you will make me cry". We went back into the classroom. Even at 5 years old we understood that lights without blackout were forbidden. I got up on Miss Essex' high chair and reached the light switch which I put on and off in a signalling motion.

We gave up and went back out into the hall. We huddled together on the floor and after a while the letterbox of the door into Bournemouth Park Road was pushed open and a voice shouted in "Is anybody there?" Jean shouted back "No". Within a short while the doors to the school were opened. In came the caretaker, an ARP Warden who had shouted through the letterbox and a policeman.

Our parents had reported us missing. The policeman took us to a police car (one of those old Wolseley cars). He had a hand held microphone and called loudly "Lost children found. Lost children found". We were delivered home. Next day our parents were summoned to the school. We had no idea of the consequences of our actions. Miss Essex resigned. The caretaker, Mr. Carter, was moved to another school and the Policeman reported to his superiors that the Education Authorities must be informed because children of 5 would not lie about staying behind after school to help their teacher and getting locked in the school. Did we tell him that? Lying was a habit Jean and I had if we thought we were in trouble. These awful consequences resulting from two lying five year olds were not known to us at the time.

Fast forward about 50 years and a visit to Essex Records. Jean and I rarely see each other but on the occasions we have met, often asked ourselves if we had remembered that story correctly. I was recruited by Ken Crowe, then curator of the Heritage Centre in Southend, to research a number of old postcards of the town. Ken had possession of more than 4,000 postcards and us volunteers were given 6 of these at a time each to research. This required me having access to Essex Records which then was in the adjoining library building next door. During my research I was flicking through index cards and saw "Bournemouth Park Road School". I decided to ask for the file and there in it was the school log covering the period in question. Miss Smith the head mistress wrote in the log usually just one line for each day. On 29th November the log read "Johnny Hall slipped and cut his chin on the toilet pan". Johnny Hall was in my class. Next day 30th November the log was 3 pages long. It was only then that I knew of the consequences, which had been recorded, and that our kind policeman's name was PC 168 Albert John Lesley Penny. Miss Smith's log report went on to explain that the version of events reported by PC Penny was wrong. Miss Essex did withdraw her resignation but left soon after. At age 7 I transferred to the all boys junior school. It was a separate building on the same site and I completed my education there until moving to senior school. I was oblivious of my reputation.

In his 1945 booklet A. P. Herbert wrote "That island of busy life at the Pier Head has been the brains of great affairs for five and a half tremendous years". He makes a plea for its preservation as a memorial to a great event in our nation's wartime history. In his book "The Thames" published in 1966, in referring to Southend Pier he states (at the top of p.148) "For its war services it should have the George Medal. It might have been made for war."

The estimated loss of merchant ships in coastal waters 1939 – 1945 was 1,431 vessels with a total tonnage of 3,768,600 tons. Volunteer merchant seamen killed was around 3,600 over about twenty nations.

Since the War

Immediately after the war Southend returned to its former glory as a day tripper's paradise. Kiss-me-quick hats, amusement arcades, pubs and funfair palaces stretched from the Pier to the Kursaal fairground. The seafront was known as Southend's Golden Mile. In fact it is less than a quarter of a mile long. It was an exciting time for us children too but we had no idea that this promenade of slot machines, fancy hats and candy floss had been the witness of great events for six years. Yours truly had something of a mis-spent youth in the amusement arcades from age 8 to 11 learning how to fiddle the mainly old Edwardian slot machines for reward with my pals from Stadium Road. Another of our skill challenges was to walk to the end of the Pier and race the train back to the shore.

London factory works' outings by charabanc were popular just after the war and thousands flocked into the town from London's Fenchurch Street and Liverpool Street stations. We were aware that a trip to Southend; getting drunk and into a fight was considered by many as 'a good day out'.

There were more than 5 million visitors a year to Southend in the years just after the war. The 1960's saw a decline and the steamship trips from the end of the Pier stopped. Maintenance of the Pier was a frequent complaint by the Council, not helped by pier fires that devastated parts of the structure, including to the old Solarium.

A Tribute to Peggy Dowie

By 1980 the Pier was in serious decline and the Council put forward a proposal for it to be demolished. Once that reached the local papers there was uproar and thousands of letters were received by the Council. Step forward one Peggy Dowie and husband Ron to whom all Southenders today owe a huge debt. Peggy and Ron organised a massive campaign which resulted in the Council reversing their proposals. They even held a two day 'Festival of the Pier'. Peggy and a band of volunteers were now working hard in the background to secure interest in Southend Pier.

In 1984 the Council committed itself to restoring the Pier and underwriting its future. Peggy Dowie would be the first to admit that she had by now become a thorn in the side of the Council and in 1985 created 'The Southend Pier Museum Foundation'. After years of hard work and with a bit of help from the Council who donated some old pier workshops, the Pier Museum was opened on 8th July 1989, exactly 100 years to the day after the new 'iron pier' had been declared open to the public. With the devoted help of family and other volunteers (Ron died in March 2012 after a long illness) Peggy continued to run the Pier Museum until recently, stepping down after 30 years.

Today there appears to be more interest in the Pier by the Council. There is a new pavilion at the end of the pier but it does not have cut-out palm trees and a tropical theme! Famous chef Jamie Oliver has a café at the end of the Pier which is the subject of a TV programme where he invites celebrities to join him there. Jamie has, I believe, some local connections.

When I talk to people about Southend Pier, the NCS and 6 years of incredible work in defence of the nation in wartime, they are usually staggered and wish to know more. It is time the population of Southend (circa 178,000) knew a truth of which they can be proud and our town receive some national recognition.

SS Richard Montogmery Wrecked on The Nore

The SS Richard Montgomery was an American Liberty ship of a type mass produced for use in WWII. She was built in Jacksonville, Florida in June 1943. Anchored off Southend in August 1944 and carrying 1,400 tonnes of munitions and explosives she was due to join a convoy to Cherbourg in France following its control under the Allies during the Battle of Normndy.

Orders for berthing the SS Richard Montgomery were given by the Harbour Master attached to NCS Southend. Instructions were to berth off the North edge of Sheerness Middle Sands. This was not done and while Captain Wilkie slept his ship drifted towards the dreaded Nore Sandbank. Other ships in the area who saw what was happening tried to alert the Montgomery using their sirens, but to no avail. The Montgomery dragged her anchor and ran aground. She was in shallow water and could not be moved.

A hazardous task of removing the explosives began but had to be abandoned when the ship broke its back. The ship remains submerged today nearly 80 years later and is a hazard to shipping. At low tide the masts of the SS Richard Montgomery are visible above the waves. There remains on board a sizeable quantity of explosives. These are finding their way into the sea and local fishermen often report dredging up bombs in their nets.

The wreck is regularly monitored but the fear is what the consequences would be of an explosion. It is assumed that this would send a tidal wave to Sheerness on one side and Southend on the other.

At a Board of Enquiry at the time, the ship's Chief Officer was unable to say why he did not wake Captain Wilkie and alert him. There was criticism of the Harbour Master's berthing orders as a result of which Captain Wilkie was restored to full duty a week later. This wartime disaster is a reminder of the difficulties faced in negotiating the Nore Sandbank to reach the North Sea.

The Nore Mutiny

In 1797 the crew of His Majesty's 90 gun ship Sandwich was seized by the crew. They persuaded other ships to join them in a fleet to 'block the Nore' and prevent trading vessels passing up the Thames to London. Their main grievance was over pay. The mutiny lasted for some time but was overcome by the navy. The ringleader, poor Richard Parker aged 30, was elected as President of the Delegates of the Fleet. He was eventually taken, tried and hanged. 400 others were court martialled.

———

Recognition has now arrived

Since writing the foregoing account there has come some very welcome recognition of wartime activity on the Pier. A large scale event took place in September 2021. "HMS Leigh - Guardian of the Thames" was planned to take place on the Pier and in the Estuary. It was a community led heritage and arts project that aims to connect people of all ages with the history of Southend Pier and is supported with National Lottery Heritage funding as well as the Arts Council and Southend Borough Council. It will be held to coincide with the 76th Anniversary of VE-Day. The event was planned for 2020 but postponed because of the Covid 19 virus pandemic which may yet postpone it further. A key organiser of the event is Southend Councillor, Beth Hooper. Go to the website HMS Leigh - Guardian of the Thames to follow the event's news and progress.

I have agreed to cooperate with Beth and her committee and hopefully my work will be in book form by then.

However, I am not done yet.

I apologise for the limits of this work in the knowledge that over the six years of NCS in Southend there were hundreds of thousands of naval and military personnel, permanent and passing through, all of whom had a story to tell. My intention is simply to draw attention, as a proud Southender, to what was a time of such importance that it should receive greater recognition. Perhaps it is time for me to make another plea to those in high office for whom this will hold national and international interest.

The tragic death by murder of Southend MP David Amess

As the result of the overwhelming sadness felt around the country and by colleagues in the House of Commons a fitting tribute to this long serving MP was made. David Amess during his life had wished and made a number of pleas in The House for Southend to be recognised for city status. That wish was generously granted by Her Majesty the Queen with heartfelt recognition everywhere of this gift.

CHARACTER PROFILES

1. A. V. ALEXANDER
1st Earl Alexander of Hillsborough KG., CH., PC., and First Lord of the Admiralty (1885 – 1965)

Albert Victor Alexander, born in Weston super Mare, was named after his father who in turn was named after Queen Victoria's nephew Albert Victor, Duke of Clarence. In 1929 he became an MP for the Co-operative Movement which was an immensely powerful organisation at that time. A. V. Alexander was to become the only Labour cabinet minister to hold the position of First Lord of the Admiralty and was a supporter of Winston Churchill in becoming the leader of the War Cabinet in WWII. Churchill himself had held the position of First Lord of the Admiralty and A. V. remained very much in his shadow but was a most diligent holder of the office. He often worked late, even sleeping in his office.

In 1942 A. V. Alexander accompanied an Arctic Convoy and in 1944 visited the Normandy beaches. This First Lord of the Admiralty may not have been a naval recruit but had the highest regard for the navy; its sailors and for the merchant navy.

When A. P. Herbert wrote his booklet entitled "The War Story of Southend Pier" A. V. Alexander wrote a tribute to the NCS in Southend. It appears on the inside front cover. As First Lord of the Admiralty A. V. Alexander visited Southend on numerous occasions during the war.

2. LIEUT. COMMANDER R. V. ALISON DSO., RN
Roger Vincent Alison b. 1885 in Glastonbury Somerset

R. V. Alison won his DSO at the Battle of Jutland for "gallantry" in his command of HMS Moresby. He was placed on the retired list in about 1920 after WWI but mobilised again in September 1938. Placed on the Southampton Harbour Board and then moved to HMS Pembroke at Chatham where he was designated for duty with NOIC Port of London. This was the beginning of Alison's NCS work. He was given the impossible task of operating the Naval Control Service from London with a sub base in Southend where the Pier had been taken over by the navy.

Alison did not see eye to eye with Naval Officer in Charge Rear Admiral Boyle and argued that he should move to Southend and that he should have control over both navy and merchant navy. The navy was at that time answerable to The Admiralty and the Merchant Navy to The Board of Trade. It was Alison who was the first the first NCS officer at Southend. He did stirling work on setting up the service but fell ill and was replaced by Capt. John Pelham Champion. The initial very difficult task of setting up in Southend was always attributed to Alison.

3. PAYMASTER LIEUT. NOWELL BAIRD OBE., RN (1889 – 1961)

born in Alverstoke, Hampshire. Nowell Baird's OBE was awarded in the 1945 New Years Honours.

Nowell Baird joined the Navy in 1907. After qualifying as a Paymaster and serving in that role for nearly eight years he was place on the retired list in 1920. When recruited for WWII service at NCS Southend Nowell Baird was here from first to last. He was ideal for NCS Southend because of his wide ranging abilities in administration. He was the base Secretary to Capt. Champion who gave him very high praise indeed on his discharge at the end of the war. Nowell Baird undertook numerous admin duties and was effectively in charge of the WRENS who had fifty officers and 150 ratings. He was an ever popular stalwart of the team that was NCS Southend.

4. LIEUT. COMMANDER I. M. BURT RNVR

I.M. Burt had a key position as Pier Head Control Officer and was stationed at the end of the Pier with an office in the Solarium. There was also an Officer of the Watch to cover the night shift making this a 24 / 7 operation organising the activities of tugs and drifters. On his staff Burt had many Norwegian and Dutch officers and one Polish officer. There was contact with Convoy Commodores and it is said that Burt kept a scrapbook full of the names of Admirals, Masters, the names of American sailors and foreign correspondents.

Believed to have come originally from Southampton, Burt settled after the war in Harcourt Avenue, Southend.

5. LIEUT. COMMANDER SIR JOSEPH GURNEY BRAITHWAITE

1st Baronet (1895 – 1958)

Joseph Gurney Braithwaite was born in Yorkshire into a Quaker family. He served in the navy with distinction in WWI at the Battle of Suvla Bay, Gallipoli and then in Palestine. After that war he became a stockbroker and a Conservative MP. Ironically his seat was Sheffield Hillsborough and was served when Labour were in power by A. V. Alexander. When Gurney Bratithwaite was MP during the war and based with NCS Southend A. V. Alexander was First Lord of The Admiralty. After the war, when Labour were back in power, A. V. Alexander won back the Hillsborough seat.

Gurney Braithwaite was a very active member of the team at NCS Southend and was No. 1 officer. He contributed actively on both convoy work and in the social events on the base as witnessed by frequent mention of him in "Spun Yarn" the NCS Journal (magazine). His other valuable contribution to the magazine were his reports on parliamentary matters under the alias "Jimmy the One". His visits to The House of Commons were by travel from Southend by train to London and by tube to Westminster.

6. JOHN PELHAM CHAMPION CBE., DSO., RN

Commodore-in-Charge Naval Control Servises Southend (1883 – 1955). John Champion was born in Edale, Derbyshire. His father was The Rev. Francis B. Champion.

At age 13 years and 10 months John Champion joined the training ship Britannia at Dartmouth. Just 3 months before him and in training at the same time was recruit Andrew Browne Cunningham who went on to become Admiral of the Fleet 1st Viscount Cunningham of Hyndhope KT., GCB., OM., DSO and two bars.

Captain Champion's DSO was earned at the Battle of Jutland in command of the destroyer Maenad. His citation reads "For gallant leadership of 2nd Division, 12th Destroyer Flotilla." With others at 2.15 a.m. they attacked an enemy Battleship Squadron. The British were heavily outnumbered. In the Maenad, on seeing the haze lift and facing the German ships Captain Champion ordered release of one of its torpedoes at a Konig Class German battleship. Following heavy fire on the 12th Flotilla the destroyer Onslaught next to the Maenad was hit. One British torpedo found its mark before they retreated.

However, still with one torpedo left, Captain Champion turned the Maenad around and went back to face the enemy. It was now 2.28 a.m. only 13 minutes after the first attack. The torpedo was released and gun crews now fired away aft of the ship. They had not previously had the chance and although 4 inch shells against German battleship armour was ineffective the crew felt better. The Maenad now headed for the Forth in Scotland.

At 5 a.m. Captain Champion saw a lot of oil and wreckage. The captain of the wrecked ship Ardent was spotted. He had been in the water for five hours and close to death. A further search revealed a Carly raft with survivors. These were from another wrecked ship the Fortune (not an apt name in the circumstances). At that point the periscope of a German submarine was sighted and a torpedo from it passed under the stern of the Maenad. After steaming round in circles at high speed they stopped to pick up eleven survivors. Another destroyer picked up a few more.

Captain John Pelham Champion's role in managing the NCS operation in Southend throughout the war is covered in the text of this book.

7. COMMANDERS IN CHIEF, THE NORE

Tribute to Admiral Sir Henry John Studholme Brownrigg in the church at Denham in Buckinghamshire

ADMIRAL SIR HENRY JOHN STUDHOLME BROWNRIGG KCB., CB., DSO.
(1882 – 1943)

C in C The Nore from January to December 1939 and therefore just a few months during the establishment of NCS Southend. Admiral Studholme Brownrigg's DSO was for distinguished service at the Battle of Jutland. After his C in C The Nore duties the Admiral volunteered himself as a commodore of Atlantic convoys out of Liverpool. On 12th January 1943 he left Liverpool en route to New York in the SS Ville de Tamatave a ship captured from the Vichy French. After eleven days at sea the ship ran into a violent storm and lost her rudder. It was not possible to reach the ship before she sank with all hands including Admiral Studholme Brownrigg. The tribute to him above is in the church at Denham in Buckinghamshire.

Admiral The Hon. Reginald Plunket-Ernle Erle Drax

ADMIRAL THE HON. REGINALD PLUNKET-ERNLE ERLE DRAX KCB., DSO.
(1880 – 1967)

Born Reginal Aylmer Ranfurly Plunkett he was often ribbed about his later long title. This Admiral's DSO was also earned at the Battle of Jutland when commanding HMS Blanche. As C in C The Nore Admiral Plunkett was in command 1940 – 1941. There was a great rapport between the Admiral and NCS Southend which he is on record as praising for their efficiency. After C in C The Nore duties Plunkett was another Admiral who volunteered to act as a commodore of Atlantic convoys. Plunkett was First and Principal Aide to George V1. Chronicled papers that he wrote are lodged at Churchill College Cambridge.

Spy cartoon of Lt. G. H. d'Olyly Lyon, United Services and England Rugby Player

ADMIRAL GEORGE HAMILTON D'OYLY LYON KCB.
was born in India (1883 1947)

Apart from his excellent naval record Admiral Lyon was known as being one of the greatest sportsmen ever in naval service. He played first class cricket for Hampshire and the navy and was capped twice for England at Rugby Union. Admiral Lyon served as C in C The Nore 1941 – 1943 and thereafter declared unfit for service. A terrible blow for a man of such previous physical and sporting ability. In 1946 George Lyon was diagnosed with pulmonary tuberculosis and disseminated sclerosis. He died in the Edward VII Sanatorium in Sussex on 20th August 1947.

Admiral John Cronyn Tovey 1st Baronet Tovey

ADMIRAL JOHN CRONYN TOVEY 1st BARONET TOVEY
GCB., KBE., DSO., DCL
(1885 1971)

Admiral John Tovey earned his DSO at the Battle of Jutland for heroic action in the destroyer Onslow as part of the 13th Flotilla of the Grand Fleet. John Tovey was the last of the WWII Commanders in Chief The Nore serving in that capacity from 1943 – 1945. Jack Tovey as he was often referred to was considered to be one of the greatest naval Admirals of his day. Very strict, religious without imposing his views and with a great sense of humour. Although not ambitious Tovey was said to make himself the best at whatever he occupied himself with. When NCS Southend celebrated its 2,000th convoy, Admiral Tovey visited to join in the celebrations and at an evening dinner congratulated the guest of honour Captain Champion. During the day he visited the pier to see the operations there.

8. REAR ADMIRAL OSWALD HENRY DAWSON, KBE., RN
(1882 – 1950)

Oswald Henry Dawson entered the navy direct from Malvern in Worcestershire. His connection with Southend NCS was in acting as Commodore of the very first Atlantic Convoy OA1 on 7th September, 1939 just four days after the declaration of war against Germany. Dawson re-entered service in the Royal Navy on 5th September, 1939 and sailed in the SS Glucester Castle two days later. From November and the rest of his wartime service he became a Commodore of Atlantic Convoys out of Liverpool which had the shore base name of HMS Eaglet.

9. PEGGY DOWIE
Champion And Saviour Of Southend Pier And Creator Of The Pier Museum

After Southend Council put forward in 1980 a proposal to demolish The Pier stating it to be a financial liability, there was uproar. A campaign was started to save the pier and harness the support of indignant locals and others farther afield. Up stepped Peggy Dowie and her husband Ron. Peggy and Ron worked hard. They created a two day Festival of the Pier and persuaded the Council to change its mind. Peggy then founded the Pier Museum Foundation. Peggy with family members and her band of volunteers ran the Pier Museum (based in an old workshops space at the entrance to the pier, given by the Council) until stepping down after 30 years. Unfortunately Ron died in March 2012 following a long illness. Peggy should be remembered in her retirement as a great champion of our town and its pier.

10. A. P. HERBERT
(Sir Alan Herbert) (1890 – 1971)

Alan Patrick Herbert was born in Elstead, Surrey. After studying law at Oxford University he served in the Navy in WW1 as a Sub. Lieut. at Gallipoli. After that war he published his book "The Secret Battle" in 1919. In 1924 Herbert joined Punch Magazine and two years later had his first theatrical success with the production of "Riverside Nights". Herbert was multi-talented as a writer, poet, lawyer and an Independent MP. He was befriended by Churchill who could recite and sing the words of a Herbert West End Musical.

In World War II and living in Teddington where he 'messed about on the river' (Upper Thames) in his boat Water Gipsy he was recruited for Thames Patrol. Water Gipsy was commandeered, painted battleship grey and mounted with a Lewis Gun. As a Petty Officer Herbert was allowed keep control of her with a small crew. His knowledge of the River Thames from Teddington to the Thames Estuary was invaluable. Who better at the end of the war to write the booklet for Southend Corporation from first-hand experience of Naval Control Service operations entitled The War Story of Southend Pier? The inspiration for this book.

AP continued to attend the House of Commons throughout the war as an important member, often called upon to conduct special meetings. Churchill had A. P. Herbert knighted. Apart from the many books written by AP over his lifetime his book simply entitled "The Thames" and his autobiography give further fascinating insight into his wartime service on the river. AP retired from the House of Commons in 1950.

11. VICE ADMIRAL SIR RICHARD LANE-POOLE
(1883 – 1971)

Sir Richard Hayden Owen Lane-Poole CB., KBE., RN was born in Richmond, Surrey. His father was an Egyptologist. Lane-Poole attended the 'Mining School' in Portsmouth and became an expert in mine laying during WW1. This expertise was of great value to the NCS in WWII when Vice Admiral Lane-Poole became Director of Demagnetization and a Commodore of Convoys. From 1936 – 1938 Lane-Pool became Rear Admiral commanding His Majesty's Australian Squadron. His brother had settled in Australia in 1916. At Southend Vice Admiral Lane-Poole became Commodore of the first convoy of the war FN1 to Methil in Scotland with 19 ships on 7th September 1939 just four days after the outbreak of war. He travelled in the collier SS Hetton.

Like Commodore John Champion, Lane-Poole was involved in convoys out of Halifax Nova Scotia to Liverpool. He stood down in 1943 with ill health but returned in July 1944 as Vice Commodore with HX 300 from Halifax to Liverpool with Destroyer escorts Whitley, Witch and the Sloop Pelican. They took two days.

Lane-Poole retired in 1945 and with his wife Sigrid then went to live in Australia.

12. NEVILE SHUTE NORWAY
(1899 – 1960)

Nevile Shute was an English novelist and aeronautical engineer born in Ealing, London (then Middlesex). Shute began his career with the de Haviland Aircraft Company moving in 1924 to Vickers Limited where he was involved as a stress engineer on the R100 Airship. In the 1930's Shute established his own company together with ex de Haviland trained A. Hessell Tiltman. It was called Airspeed Limited. They created the Airspeed Oxford training aircraft used by the RAF and others and 8,500 were built. Shute as a part time yachtsman became a Royal Naval Volunteer Reservist with the rank of sub-lieutenant and finishing as a Lieutenant Commander.

In his early years of working for the Admiralty, designing war weapons he spent his evenings writing and establishing himself as a leading novelist. Many of his books were later to become films i.e. On the Beach and A Town Like Alice.

As a writer Shute was recruited as a war correspondent, linking with the U.S. Navy in Southend and travelling with them to Normandy. His war correspondent record of that experience is in 4 part account lodged with his Foundation Papers in Cambridge. After the war Shute moved to Melbourne, Australia where he continued a life of adventure including becoming a racing driver. He died there aged 60 in 1960.

13. CAPTAIN A. S. MAY, MVO., OBE., RN
(1885 – 1947)

Archibold Seaburne May was born into a naval family in Southsea, Hampshire. His MVO Knighthood was awarded for personal assistance to H. M. King George V. Captain May arrived in Southend on 1st September 1939 to replace Captain E. H. Martin, Naval Officer in Command who had fallen sick and was retired from the service. Captain May had an excellent service record. He was an expert in all matters to do with mines having commenced at the Mining School in Portsmouth early in his naval career. In Southend he was made Chief of Staff to Captain John Champion. It was to Captain May that Captain Champion turned on the morning of his amazing hunch that this night would be the night the Germans might decide to attack The Pier and Anchorage. Captain May could be relied upon to obtain men and guns to mount a defence of The Pier if Captain Champion's hunch was right. The Luftwaffe came and attacked that night but such a spirited defence was put up that they were persuaded that The Pier was heavily defended and never attacked again leaving NCS operations to continue for the entire period of the war and to keep The Thames open.

Captain May suffered terribly from two chronic ailments. He had osteoarthritis of the spine for 10 years and frequently suffered with tonsillitis. Sadly in 1947 he died of a heart attack only one and a half hours after tonsilitis surgery.

Captain John Pelham Champion with his team and his dog

13. SUB. LIEUT MARTIN SOLOMON RNVR
(1915 – 1956)

Martin Solomon was a hero of Dunkirk in command of a number of Leigh cockle boats. Read his amazing story as written in the first Spun Yarn magazine February 1941. For his services he was awarded the DSC. He went on to earn a second DSC for gallantry when later rescuing many men from Tobruk when he was stationed in Egypt including saving 100 men from a schooner hit by a German shell. However, here is the equally remarkable detail of his life before the war.

Martin Herbert Solomon was born in Kensington, London in 1915. His father was Col. Robert Solomon MC, a lawyer and a prominent British Zionist until his death at age 59 just before the start of WWII. Martin's mother died in 1922 aged 34 years. We have no details of Martin's first marriage which was in August 1949. Martin was educated at Rugby and Christ's College Cambridge. He became a theatre manager and producer in London working on shows at The Savoy and Kingsway theatres. At The Arts Theatre Martin managed James Mason who was just about to ascend into Hollywood stardom. He also managed John Mills and Michael Wilding who many do not know was born in Leigh-on-Sea. Martin Solomon enrolled in the Royal Naval Volunteer Supplementary Reserve in 1938. Following just four days of training at HMS King Alfred in Portsmouth he was one of only four officers to graduate. All four joined the Thames Naval Control at Southend and were billeted in The Palace Hotel.

Martin continued to serve with distinction in Egypt and the Eastern Mediterranean mainly in anti-submarine motor torpedo boats. He was promoted to Commanding Office of 6th MTB Flotilla in December 1940 and is believed to have been working with the Intelligence Services.

After his many wartime exploits Martin Solomon became an exporter and a director for Pye Marine Radio. In 1953 he was re-engaged by the Navy for work in Korea.

In March 1956 Martin married Vida Bendix, a Spanish-born Norwegian cabaret star, sometimes knows as 'Miss Freckles'. However, just three months after they were married he died in mysterious circumstances in the Crillon Hotel in Madrid. Being Jewish his body was flown back to England for immediate burial.